SELECTIVE TROUT

SELECTIVE TROUT

A Dramatically New and Scientific Approach to Trout Fishing on Eastern and Western Rivers

by
DOUG SWISHER and CARL RICHARDS
illustrated
Preface by Joe Brooks

CROWN PUBLISHERS, INC., NEW YORK

For Marlene and Alecia,
whose patience, understanding, and inspiration were necessary
to make this book possible

LIBRARY OF CONGRESS CATALOG CARD NUMBER: 78–147342
PRINTED IN THE UNITED STATES OF AMERICA
PUBLISHED SIMULTANEOUSLY IN CANADA BY GENERAL
PUBLISHING COMPANY LIMITED

Third Printing, June, 1971

All photographs and line drawings by the authors

Contents

> Color photographs of mayflies, nymphs,
> and artificials   following page 120

Acknowledgments

WE WISH TO THANK the following persons, each of whom contributed so generously to our work:

Joe Brooks, truly the world's number-one fly-fisherman, for his insistence upon perfection;

Art Flick for the inspiration provided not only by his angling accomplishments and contributions, but also by being Art Flick;

Ernie Schwiebert for the identification of some Eastern species and the inspiration provided by his many contributions to the world of fly-fishing;

Vince Marinaro for his pioneer work in terrestrial fishing and in new-pattern innovations;

Justin Leonard, George Edmunds, and Steven Jensen for their invaluable assistance in identifying species of aquatic insects across the entire country;

Fred Olson for his assistance in the collection and identification of both Eastern and Midwestern insects;

Freeman Haskins for his mechanical talents, which we utilized for the construction of lab and field equipment;

Ronald Powell for his assistance in collecting Eastern species;

Dr. Will Godfrey for his help in collecting Western species;

Lefty Kreh and Norm Le Gallee for their invaluable contributions to our photographic efforts;

Rod Towsley for many words of encouragement and inspiration.

Preface

by Joe Brooks

IN MY WORK as an outdoor writer I have met many great anglers and flytiers. Outstanding among them are the authors of this book. I first encountered Doug Swisher and Carl Richards while fishing the Main Branch of the Au Sable River in Michigan a few years ago. These two men, one a plastics salesman, one a dentist, started out as fishing partners with a common enthusiasm for fly-fishing for trout. They soon found that they also shared a keen interest in the life of the aquatic insects on which trout feed and a great curiosity about how to tie artificial flies which would match the demanding fly hatches on some of Michigan's famous trout streams. They also had a mutual interest in photography. From this basis they developed into entomologist-anglers, zealously collecting the natural insects at the various stages of their development, observing and recording and photographing their growth and changes—and then trying to tie flies which would match these insects from the trout's point of view.

From their initial investigations on the Au Sable, Doug and Carl extended their coverage to many of the most famous trout streams in North America, following the same system: collecting, photographing, and studying the local fly hatches, then working out their patterns for artificial flies and fishing them to prove their worth.

Out of their work came one of the great dry-fly discoveries of North American fly-fishing history, the "no-hackle dry fly," a design which is almost entirely at variance with the past trends of fly tying. It was my privilege to be the first to report on this new development, in an article published in *Outdoor Life* magazine in August 1970.

That article was a summary of the chief points of only one part of the investigations and discoveries of these two innovative anglers. In *Selective Trout,* anglers and flytiers will find a complete record of their work in the identification of our American flies. Their clear, simplified methods have opened the way for the dry-fly fishing fraternity, both beginners and veterans, to have a look at these natural flies, and to benefit immeasurably in their own fishing and fly tying by a more complete knowledge of the insects upon which trout feed.

CHAPTER 1

Science and Selectivity

THE SELECTIVITY OF TROUT has always been the most difficult and challenging of the numerous problems that confront the fly-fisherman. Now and in the future, with fishing pressure increasing at a tremendous rate, the problem will become even more acute. The growing popularity of fly-fishing, combined with the activities of the great dam builders, will continue to increase this pressure in the coming years. Each season we find more and more fishermen wading our favorite pools, and paralleling this trend, we find our friend the trout becoming more and more selective. With the advent of special fishing regulations and an increase in the number of no-kill areas, trout that are caught more than once become even more selective and leader shy.

Even before the recent deluge of fishermen, however, there was a need for new patterns and techniques to fool those selective risers. How many times have you been involved in that typical situation—dozens of fish feeding all around, but you get nothing except refusals? At almost all of these frustrating times the problem is having the *wrong* fly—a fly that is probably *too large, too bushy,* and obviously *very unrealistic in appearance.*

For us, having the *right* fly for a given hatch is 100 percent more effective and much more satisfying than fumbling along with something "fairly close." The *right* fly is the one that resembles the natural so closely that the fish *seem* to prefer it over the real thing. A good imitation can mean the difference between thirty fish and no fish on a given day. Many of the old standard patterns just do not work well during these selective situations. If the fish move for them at all, they drift up, take a long leisurely look and then turn disdainfully away.

Anglers are eager to blame their inability to take fish on a variety of factors. Some excuses include, "My tippet was too heavy," "My casting was bad today," "I couldn't get a drag-free float." In most cases, the real reason was having the wrong fly. Since one of the most common is the tippet excuse, we did some experimenting in this area, using tippets that were much larger and stiffer than recommended; we scored just as well as we did with the smaller tippets, *when* we had the right fly on. For example, on the tiny *Tricorythodes* spinner, we've used 4X and 5X tippets without *any* drop-off in success.

But before even a realistic imitation will raise a trout, it is necessary to know which fly the fish are feeding on. The Au Sable River in Michigan and other even-flowing rivers like it all over the country have many different species of aquatic insects hatching every day of the season. These rich rivers have a high lime content that results in tremendous hatches; often two or three different species will be on the water at the same time. On these prolific waters, the fisherman must not only match the hatch but also discover *which* hatch the fish are taking. It can be difficult but certainly it is never dull.

To make matters even more complicated, individual fish may exhibit an individual preference during a multiple hatch. This phenomenon is due to the varying character of the stream below the lines of drift. Correspondingly, each nymphal type requires its own kind of water habitat, and, as a result, higher concentrations of specific species occur in specific areas.

Hand magnifier

An observant and creative angler should be able to conquer these selective situations. During peak emergence periods, the trout usually throw caution to the wind by boldly coming out from their hiding places and feeding voraciously. This is the fulfillment of every fly-fisherman's "dream"—his magic moment—and he should make the most of it. It is also the moment of truth. For at this moment, with the stream pocketed with feeding trout, an angler's skill is given its sternest test.

After experiencing many of these frustrating slack-line episodes, we decided to attempt a logical and scientific approach to the problem by making a closer study of the trout's food and his feeding habits. We were aware of the aquatic insects trout feed on and the standard patterns used to imitate those insects, but since standard dressings were so consistently ineffective during periods of heavy feeding and high selectivity, we wanted to examine the situation more closely.

The average fly-fisherman is a fairly observant and creative fellow. He is aware of the floating and flying creatures around him and he is also conscious of the relationship between these graceful winged creatures and the trout's diet. He is even able to create or purchase an imitation that closely resembles the size, color, and shape of the natural he observed—or *thought* he observed! However, observation is where the trouble usually begins. To "observe" sounds like a very simple and basic process, but when it comes to observing aquatic insects, more than a casual glance is required. Most fishermen that claim to know "what the hatch is" have merely watched an insect fly or float by at a distance of at least three or four feet. In many cases, when an insect is caught and observed at close range, preferably with some magnification, it will look much different from when it is floating past your rod tip or flying overhead. The first step in our quest for a solution to the problem, then, was to begin collecting aquatic insects—mostly mayflies, caddis flies, and stone flies—and then to observe them under magnification.

Each of us interprets color differently, so we decided the best way to accumulate the desired information was through close-up photography, or, to be more specific, photomacrography. Our goal was to produce true color photographs of each stage of all the most important aquatic insects. And, just as important, we wanted to magnify these photographs enough to obtain a trout's-eye view of each insect. The reason for wanting a magnified view is quite simple. If we hold a fly, or any object, for that matter, at a distance of only three or four inches from our eyes, it is completely out of focus. It will be blurred and appear as a very dim and indistinct form. In order to bring it into focus and see it clearly, a magnifying lens of two to three power is required. Since trout inspect drifting flies at this same close range, it would thus seem obvious that we must use similar magnification factors in our photography.

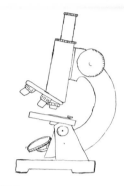

High-power microscope

Not only did we obtain ideas for improved patterns from the pictures, but we also accumulated much valuable data and experience while collecting the specimens. We automatically found out how, when, and where each insect emerges during the collection process. This information, in turn, was used to develop hatching calendars, and it provided many new ideas on technique. By using the hatching calendar, the new patterns, and the how, when, and where information, it became possible to apply an orderly scientific approach to fly-fishing that would greatly increase one's catch per hour and reduce sharply the number of those baffling moments of "unmatched hatches." The plan worked for us—and it can for you.

For the expert, we offer new and interesting changes in some of the old standard patterns that have "supposedly" withstood the test of time. For the beginner, we offer a simplified and logical introduction into the world of fly-fishing—with an examination of the principal aquatic and terrestrial insects forming the trout's diet, emergence calendars that can be adapted for use in any section of the country, full instructions for tying the new patterns, and large full-color photographs to help identify and imitate the insects.

We have only scratched the surface of this sport that deals with the whims and fancies of the trout. Many chapters and volumes have yet to be written, but we hope we have opened up a new avenue of thinking and have created a fresh, systematic, scientific approach.

CHAPTER 2

Collecting, Photographing, Identifying

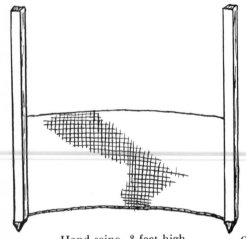

Hand seine—3 feet high

THE EQUIPMENT USED in our study falls into three general categories: collection, photographic, and identification. Methods and equipment required for the accumulation of specimens need not be complicated or expensive; what can be done is limited only by individual ingenuity.

Many nymphs and winged insects can be collected by hand, while others must be obtained with the aid of various kinds of seines and nets. For the collection of underwater specimens, a simple hand seine can be used. This device consists of a strip of window screen connected to two wooden handles. A piece of screen thirty inches long by twenty inches wide attached to three-foot handles is quite functional and yet easy to carry in the car. To use this seine, the collector stands in the water facing downstream, holding the screen at arm's length, tight against the bottom of the stream. When the bottom material is disturbed and dislodged, usually by digging with the feet, both specimens and debris will flow into the seine. The nymphs can then be either picked off by hand or washed into a suitable container. Many other types of seines can be devised, depending on the whims of the collector. For example, a simple kitchen strainer attached to the end of a long handle is useful for catching some of the free-swimming nymphs that occupy the deeper runs, while a screen-wire scap net of rugged construction is helpful in obtaining the muck-burrowing nymphs.

After the underwater specimens have been captured, they should be put in a suitable container that will keep them alive during transportation. We have found that insulated buckets molded out of foam are very suitable; small thermos bottles and even glass jars containing ice cubes are also practical. Be very sure to put all specimens in the stream water they came from, for the use of regular tap water will sometimes kill them in a short period of time.

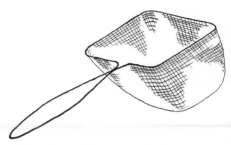

Hand aquarium net—8 inches long

Collection of the winged stages, duns and spinners, can be more varied and difficult, partially owing to their short period of availability. The ideal time to capture freshly hatched duns is immediately after they've emerged and are floating along on the surface. This is the time that we all want to be on the stream anyway. It is usually a simple task to scoop up a few floating duns with the aid of a small aquarium hand net. In fact, one of these nets should be a permanent part of the equipment carried in the fishing vest. It may look easy to snatch a floating fly from the water's surface with the bare hand, but at least for the smaller specimens, it is very difficult. Spinners can be captured in the same manner as the duns when they fall into the water after mating. Both duns and spinners can be found in such places as bushes and trees along the streamside, on bridge abutments and docks, on weeds growing along the bank, and on cabin walls. One of our favorite spots is at a service station near the banks of the Au Sable River in Grayling, where duns and spinners are attracted by the bright lights. Spinners can also be caught with long-handled butterfly nets as they swarm overhead.

Wire scap net—4 feet long

Originally, all of our collecting was done at the stream, usually during a fishing expedition. However, it soon became evident that something more was required to facilitate the study. We could not possibly be on the stream during each emergence to sample all of the hatches, so we decided to transport nymphs from the stream to our homes, where they were put into aquariums to complete their growth. This allowed us to keep track of most of the major hatches every single day, not just during periodic fishing trips. Of even greater importance was the tremendous advantage gained for our photographic efforts. It is much easier to keep the camera ready in the one spot it is needed than to tote it along on each fishing excursion, where constantly varying light and weather conditions exist. A freshly hatched dun can be quickly removed from the aquarium and placed on the miniature photographing stage before color changes begin. There is no wind or rain to contend with, the light source can remain constant, and much of the guesswork is eliminated. Nymphs can be photographed right through the aquarium walls and their habits thoroughly observed.

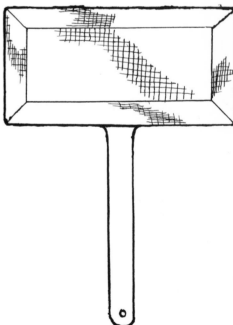

Other advantages provided by the aquarium are faster growth of the insect and, perhaps most important, more fishing time for the fisherman. By being indoors during the winter months, nymphal growth is greatly accelerated, thereby producing hatches two to three months early. Hen-

A few of the aquariums used
by the authors

Microscopes, cameras, and
other equipment in the authors' lab

dricksons, for example, which normally hatch in the stream during late April and May, will come as early as February in the aquarium. This means that picture-taking and identification can be concluded far in advance of the natural time schedule, and this, of course, results in more fishing time.

Some nymphs, such as *Siphlonurus* and *Isonychia* have difficulty in adapting to aquarium life, but most of the important species can be reared very well in standard tropical fish aquariums with filters. Most of our aquariums range from five to forty gallons in size; a water temperature of approximately 65° F. is maintained. We seine nymphs from many locations around the state and country so that we can identify as many species as possible. To date, we have obtained insects from most of the important trout states including Michigan, Montana, New York, Idaho, Wyoming, Colorado, Vermont, New Jersey, and Pennsylvania. Some of the more important rivers we have studied include the Beaverkill and Esopus of New York, the Paulinskill and Pequest of New Jersey, Paradise Creek of Pennsylvania, the Madison, Yellowstone, and Big Hole of Montana, Henrys Fork of the Snake in Idaho, and the Au Sable in Michigan.

In order to produce the pictures we desired, it was necessary to obtain equipment that would enable us to make photomacrographs. The pictures produced by photomacrography permit detailed and precise study of minute objects. In our case, the minute objects are aquatic insects. Generally speaking, photomacrography is a process by which we can record on film subjects that are smaller than the resulting film image. Specifically, for our study, we can say that images recorded from actual size to approximately four times actual size are regarded as photomacrographs. An additional requirement is that a camera lens is used instead of supplementary optics such as those of a microscope.

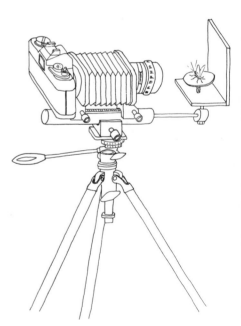

The amount of equipment needed for photomacrography is not great and consists principally of a camera, a lens, and a medium for protracting the lens out from the camera body. For our work we chose a 35-mm SLR body, a 50-mm F/3.5 lens, and a bellows. Other accessories include a tripod, coupler, Polaroid filter, and cable release. Most specimens are photographed on a small stage that is securely attached to the bellows. Depending on the color of the insect and the effect desired, both stage and background can easily be changed to suit the situation. The entire photographic setup should be sturdy and as free of vibration as possible. A large number of different films can be used for this type of work and each has its own characteristics. Probably the most important aspect of picture-taking is to know your equipment inside out and to chart all results.

The identification of aquatic insects is a highly interesting process; it can also be quite difficult. Identification at the family and genus levels is usually quite routine, but determination of the final species can be puzzling and uncertain. There are so many similarities among closely related species that it can become extremely difficult to recognize the dissimilarities. Some of the basic equipment required for the identification process includes a low-power wide-field microscope, scalpel, forceps, dissecting needles, eyedroppers, glass slides, storage vials and racks, various hand magnifiers, and reference books. Most of our identifications were made from three publications: *Mayflies of Michigan Trout Streams* by Justin W. and Fannie A. Leonard, *The Mayflies, or Ephemeroptera, of Illinois* by B. D. Burks, and *Aquatic Insects of California*, edited by R. L. Usinger.

Our equipment is mostly uncomplicated and inexpensive. Much of it, such as nets, seines, and stages can be designed and fashioned by the individual; other items, though, such as the camera and microscope may be quite expensive and can be mastered only with practice.

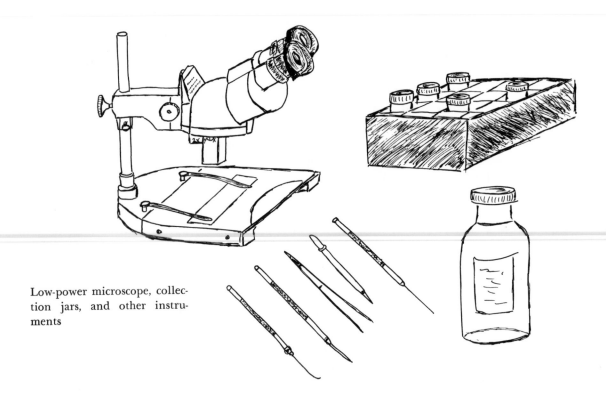

Low-power microscope, collection jars, and other instruments

CHAPTER 3

The Need for Realistic Imitation

The single most overriding problem the fly-fisherman must deal with is procuring an artificial fly that will gull the trout into thinking it is a natural insect. The single most difficult period for accomplishing deception is during the rise to a hatch of naturals. During this period the fish become familiar with a specific insect after feeding on it over and over. The finest leader, smoothest casts, and the most beautiful drag-free floats are all useless if the trout is not duped into thinking that the artificial is the real thing.

Many anglers experience success only when the fish are not selective, at those times when rise activity is sparse or nonexistent. Their predicament is usually due to the unrealistic appearance of the standard patterns of trout flies. These standard patterns just do not simulate, to the trout, their view of the naturals. Realistic and effective patterns for specific hatches make it possible to hook and release many more trout, even during the most selective rises.

Trout feeding habits vary greatly depending on the velocity of water and type of stream the fish inhabit. All very small trout feed mainly on aquatic

". . . standard patterns just do not simulate, to the trout, their view of the naturals."

insects; as they grow larger, though, other fish, such as minnows and smaller trout, become increasingly important to their diet. This cannibalistic tendency is accelerated on rapid rivers like the lower Madison and on streams with little insect life. Much energy is required to chase food through fast, heavy current, so the prey must be large enough to be worthwhile. On these swift streams, larger trout may not feed heavily on small insects. Thus, the dry-fly angler will generally profit more if he concentrates on those rivers where the hatch produces consistent and reliable feeding activity.

The types of streams that are conducive to the dry fly and to selective rising trout are:

(1) *Slow pools, interspaced with riffles or rapids;* examples are the Beaverkill and the Neversink in the East; Rock Creek, Yellowstone, the North and South Fork of the Platte, and the Upper Madison in the West.

(2) *Uniform flow, unbroken water;* examples are the limestone rivers of the East such as the Letort and Big Springs in Pennsylvania, the Au Sable in Michigan, and the spring creeks of Idaho and Montana, such as Henrys Fork of the Snake and the twenty to thirty Gallatin River Valley spring creeks.

These types of waters are quite common, and it is in them that we find our extraordinarily selective trout. On these sleek rivers, large trout will remain "insect eaters" much longer because they can hover and sip small bites without expending large amounts of energy in the slow, easy flow. The more rapid the current, the larger the insect must be to lure the fish up to the surface. Many rivers have fine hatches of very small mayflies all season long; but if the water is too fast they are not usually of prime importance. On the more ideal fly water, such as the placid limestone and spring creeks, large fish can and do feed well on even the smallest mayflies. In these waters, the fish get a more leisurely look at their food and have good "close vision." This enables them to differentiate between the tremendous variety of flotsam and jetsam blown and washed into a river, and the small, live, naturally camouflaged aquatic insects floating by them. Therefore, fish in these slower and more fertile waters become ultraselective during a hatch, due to the long observation time available to them.

On quiet rivers, trout often seem to prefer very small insects, ignoring much larger ones that may be hatching simultaneously. This is usually because the small flies are much more numerous. Since tiny mayflies are more difficult for the angler to see than large ones, he may erroneously believe the larger fly to be more prevalent and important. Occasionally, when trout are feeding on very large naturals, they seem to lose their native caution and hit almost any concoction. This phenomenon may account for some individual opinions that realistic patterns are not important or necessary. However, we feel that, as the size of the natural decreases, the selectivity of the trout actually appears to increase and become more critical. When fishing a #28 hatch, for example, a 1-mm variation from the natural means at least a 30 percent dimensional error—which of course is disastrous and results in nothing but refusals from the trout. Good fish often gorge on these very tiny naturals, and in our experience realistic imitation is absolutely essential in these critical situations for any consistent success. Also, it is important to bear in mind that on fertile rivers small flies comprise the real bulk of the trout's diet. The minute species hatch in far greater numbers and with much more consistency than the larger mayflies.

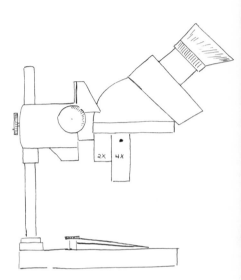

The major aquatic insects trout feed on, in their usual order of importance, are:

(1) Mayflies—upwings, *Ephemeroptera*
(2) Caddis flies—downwings, tent wings, *Tricoptera*
(3) Stone flies—downwings, flat wings, *Plecoptera*
(4) Midges—downwings, glassy wings, aquatic *Diptera*

Mayflies have wings which, when folded at rest, are upright. They are the only aquatic insects with upright wings and, as such, are easily recognized. Mayflies are by far the most important aquatic insects. They come in all sizes from #4 to #28.

On some rivers, especially below impoundments, caddis flies surpass mayflies for numbers and availability. Caddis flies have wings that are folded down and "tentlike" in an inverted V when the insect is at rest. Most caddis flies are size #14 to #20. It is usually difficult for the angler to identify the type of insect hatching by watching them fly over the river. You must catch one and examine it *at rest, in your hand:* we cannot emphasize this enough!

Catch one and examine it closely or the chances are you will be fooled. A fluttering caddis can resemble a stone fly or mayfly at a distance.

Stone flies are next in importance. Most species prefer fast, rocky water and hatch by crawling onto some object such as a rock or a log. They are taken by trout mainly on their egg-laying flights. Stone flies have flat wings when at rest. They vary in size from the exceedingly large salmon fly of the Western rivers to tiny #20s, though the most common size is #14 to #18. Yellow is their most common color.

On many quiet waters, midges are of prime interest, and are equally as important as caddis flies. They are very small, #18 to #28, often much smaller, but fish do feed on them enthusiastically and these periods offer exciting, light-tackle fishing. Midges have flat glassy wings and are true flies.

The fly-fisherman who knows what is hatching and has realistic imitations will consistently be more effective than the angler relying on trial-and-error methods. In the following chapters we will go into the detailed life cycle of these insects, their emergence characteristics, and how to imitate them successfully.

CHAPTER 4

Mayflies—The Upwings

THE UPWINGS, or mayflies, form the group of aquatic insects that make up the order Ephemeroptera. Well over five hundred different species exist on the North American continent. Four stages—egg, nymph, subimago (dun), and imago (spinner)—comprise the complete life cycle of the mayfly. Nymphs are the immature forms that live on the river bottom, in weeds, under rocks, in sand and gravel, and in muck banks along the stream's edge. Subimagos are the winged form that emerges from the nymphal case; they float along on the water's surface, drying their wings, and then fly away to a sheltered resting place. The imagos are the second winged stage that results from the final molt. After shedding their skin, they return to the stream where mating, egg laying, and death complete the cycle.

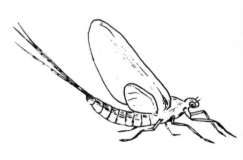

In some species, this cycle can be as short as five or six weeks, while some of the large ephemerids, such as *Hexagenia*, require a period of two years before maturity is reached. Some of the small *Baetis* flies mature from egg to adult in four or five months, which allows two broods per year of the same species. Still other flies, such as *Baetis vagans*, have an overlapping series of broods: a six-month cycle during the warmer part of the year and a nine-month cycle during the winter. In general, however, most species have a one-year life cycle. Depending on water temperature and conditions,

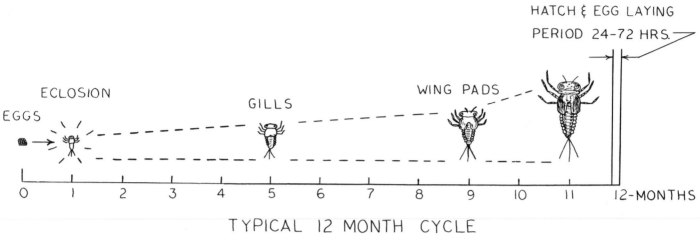

HATCH & EGG LAYING
PERIOD 24-72 HRS.

ECLOSION

EGGS

GILLS

WING PADS

0 1 2 3 4 5 6 7 8 9 10 11 12-MONTHS

TYPICAL 12 MONTH CYCLE

**COMPLETE LIFE CYCLE
OF THE MAYFLY**

most mayfly eggs hatch within a period of one to four weeks. Immediately after eclosion, when the nymph hatches from the egg, the nymphal evolution begins. At the conclusion of each stage of development, the nymph molts or sheds its outer skin which is composed mainly of chitin. The period between any two consecutive molts is called an instar. During nymphal life, most mayflies pass through an average of twenty to thirty instars which range from only a few days apart, at first, to up to two weeks toward the end. Usually, after ten instars, the gills begin to develop and at fifteen instars the wing cases become visible. The later instars give evidence of the developing adult characteristics such as the wings, eggs, and genitalia. Practically all species of mayfly nymphs utilize microscopic algae and aquatic vegetation as their food source. Only a few, such as *Isonychia* and *Metreturus* are either partially or completely predacious on other insect forms.

The body of the mayfly nymph is made up of three main parts: head, thorax, and abdomen. Main features of the head include compound eyes situated on each side, three simple eyes (or ocelli) arranged in a triangle between the compound eyes, the antennae that lie on top and toward the front of the head, and the complicated mouth parts below. The thorax is made up of three elements: the prothorax, the mesothorax, and the metathorax. The prothorax lies directly behind the head and bears the front pair of legs. The mesothorax is the middle and largest segment of the thorax; it bears the middle pair of legs and the fore wing pads. Both the hind pair of legs and hind wing pads are borne by the metathorax. The abdomen is comprised of ten segments of which from four to seven bear gills at their posterolateral corners. All mayfly nymphs are strictly aquatic and respire by means of gills that can vary immensely in shape and size. Gills are either threadlike (filiform), platelike (lamelliform), or some combination of the two. The tenth or terminal segment of the abdomen bears either two (rarely) or three slender tails.

Hexagenia limbata,
photographed from underwater

The various types of mayfly nymphs are each well adapted to specific aquatic habitats as illustrated by the following list.

(1) burrowing — sand and gravel, mud

Ephemera
Hexagenia

(2) gravel and rubble

Ephemerella
Paraleptophlebia
Baetis
Rithrogena
Epeorus
Pseudocloeon

(3) underside of stones

Stenonema
Heptagena

(4) submerged plant beds

Baetis
Callibaetis

(5) leaf drift and detritus (nonburrowing)

Ephemerella
Stenonema
Heptagenia

(6) detritus (little or no current)

Tricorythodes
Brachycercus
Caenis
Ephemerella
Baetisca
Leptophlebia
Stenonema

(7) free swimming — quiet water

Siphlonurus
Cloeon

moderate to fast water

Isonychia
Siphoplecton

The nymphs of each species have their own time and method of emergence. For example, *Siphlonurus* and *Isonychia* nymphs leave the water by crawling onto sticks, stems of plants, logs, or stones where the nymphal skin is shed and left behind. This process is fairly slow, requiring four or five minutes. *Hexagenia* nymphs, on the other hand, come to the surface of the water, split their nymphal skin, and then the subimago emerges quickly. After a short rest on the shed epicuticle, it is ready for flight. This entire sequence takes only about two minutes. Some species cast off their nymphal integument underwater and struggle to the surface where bedraggled wings must be dried before flight can occur. In general, however, the nymphs of most species rise to the surface where the nymphal skin splits and the dun emerges. As soon as the wings are dried sufficiently, the newly hatched subimago takes to the air and finds a resting place for the final molt.

In this first winged stage, the typical mayfly has two pairs of upright wings, with the anterior pair being much larger than the hind pair. A few species—*Cloeon, Pseudocloeon, Tricorythodes, Brachycercus,* and *Caenis*—lack these hind wings. Wings in the dun stage are semiopaque and display underdeveloped venation, while the bodies tend to be dull in appearance as compared to the imago stage. The adult characteristics, such as eyes,

Siphlonurus and *Isonychia* nymphs crawl onto sticks, stems, logs, or stones, where the nymphal skin is shed slowly

Hexagenia nymphs split their nymphal skin on the surface, and then the subimago quickly emerges

Epeorus nymphs emerge underwater

DUN   SPINNER

FINAL MOLT

DUN FLIES TO RESTING PLACE

SWARMING, MATING AND EGG LAYING

EMERGENCE

EGGS SINK TO BOTTOM COMPLETING CYCLE

NYMPH

| 0 | 2 | 4 | 6 | 8 | 10 | 12 | 14 | 16 | 18 | 20 | 22 | 24 |

TYPICAL 24 HOUR CYCLE

tails, and legs can be observed, constricted and compressed, under the subimaginal skin. This condition can last from only a few minutes to several days, depending on the species and weather conditions. *Hexagenia,* for example, takes three days or more to transform into the spinner stage, while *Tricorythodes* usually makes the final molt within minutes after emergence. For most species the time between emergence and the final molt is about twenty-four hours. Ephemeroptera is the only order of insects that undergoes this second stage of development between nymph and final adult.

The imago, or spinner, is usually quite different in appearance from the subimago. The true mayfly adult has a smooth and shiny body and often displays coloration that varies radically from the dun. It is often difficult to believe that dun and spinner belong to the same species. Tails of the imago often become much longer and the wings become clear and hyaline with fully developed venation. Legs and eyes generally become longer and larger, especially in the male.

The reproduction process normally occurs soon after the final molt has been completed. Mating swarms are composed of male spinners, with an occasional female that flies into the multitude to secure a mate. Once paired, the male uses his long forelegs to hold the thorax of the female and also curls his abdomen into position to make contact with the eggs. In this position, with the larger female supporting both insects, they fly away from the swarm to complete copulation. After the fertilization process has been fulfilled, the female deposits her eggs and dies shortly thereafter.

METHODS OF
DEPOSITING EGGS

Ephemeridae spinner

Stenonema, Leptophlebia, and *Siphlonurus*

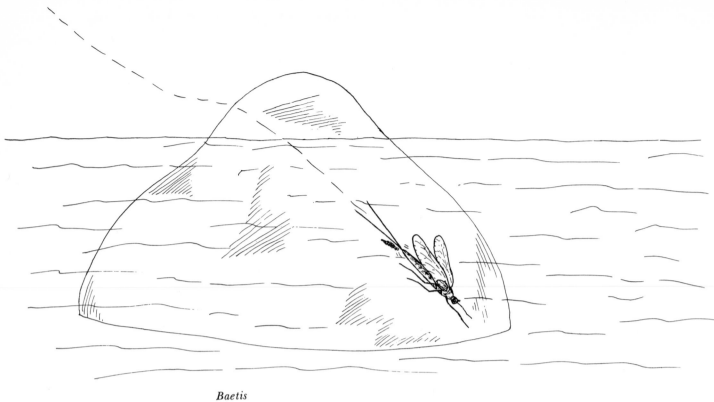

Baetis

Ephemerella

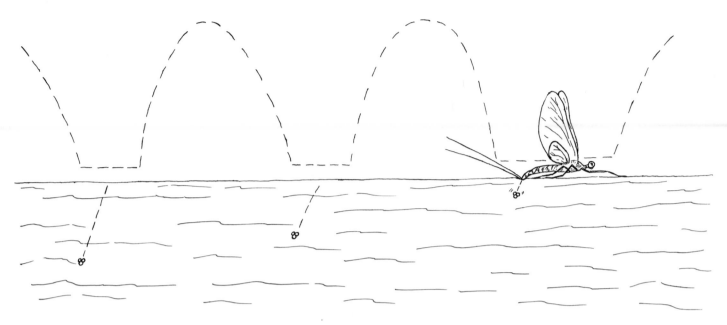

Heptagenia

The females deposit their eggs in a number of distinct ways. Females of *Heptagenia* land on the water, and while riding the current for a short distance, extrude part of their eggs into the stream. They then fly over the water for a few minutes and return again to deposit more eggs. This process is repeated until all of the eggs are extruded; they then float downstream in the spent position.

The females of such genera as *Ephemerella* form their eggs in a round mass beneath the tip of the abdomen. Then they fly close to the water's surface and suddenly dip down to break the surface film and release the entire egg sac into the stream. The eggs rapidly sink to the bottom where they stick to stones or other objects.

Females of *Baetis* species land on a stone, log, or some other object protruding from the stream and then crawl beneath the surface to deposit their eggs. In some species of *Stenonema*, *Leptophlebia*, and *Siphlonurus* the females dip the end of their abdomen into the surface of the water at intervals as they fly low over the stream. The dipping action allows a few eggs to be washed off at a time until they are all deposited. Females of the Ephemeridae family, such as *Ephemera simulans* and *Hexagenia limbata*, merely land on the water's surface and extrude all of their eggs at once. They remain on the surface with their wings flush in the film until they drown or are eaten by a fish.

Knowledge of the life cycle of mayflies can obviously be of tremendous value to the angler. For example, it is plain that the trout have four good opportunities to feed on the various stages of most mayflies—as a nymph on the bottom or on the way up; as an emerging dun slightly under or in the surface film; as a dun drifting on the surface; and as a spinner after it falls back into the water. This requires at least four patterns of artificials for many species, and sometimes more if the males and females are very dissimilar. The life cycle varies among the many Ephemeroptera and these differences are extremely important. For example, knowing that the sub-

1- NYMPH HEAVY WIRE OR WEIGHTED–FISH ON BOTTOM–USE SINKING LINE	2- NYMPH HEAVY WIRE — SINK, THEN RISE TO SURFACE — "WIGGLE NYMPH"	3- EMERGER MEDIUM WIRE – NYMPHAL BODY– WINGS SHORT – FISH SUBSURFACE	4- EMERGER LIGHT WIRE – NYMPHAL BODY– LONGER WINGS– FISH IN FILM	5- EMERGER LIGHT WIRE– DUN BODY – WINGS SLANTED FISH IN FILM	6- DUN LIGHT WIRE– WINGS UPRIGHT– NO–HACKLE OR PARADUN TYPE

EMERGENCE SEQUENCE AND POSSIBLE PATTERNS

imagos of *Tricorythodes* immediately molt into spinners indicates the simultaneous presence of both duns and spinners—which, in turn, means that you have to determine which stage the fish are feeding on.

The various types of mayflies have a wide range of requirements in relation to the kind of water they need. Some mayflies like fast gravel runs (*Ephemerella subvaria*); some like submerged plant beds (*Baetis* species); some like detritus with little or no current (*Tricorythodes* species); some like to burrow in sand and gravel (*Ephemera simulans*); and some like to burrow in mud (*Hexagenia limbata*). Others, such as *Cloeon* and *Siphlonurus,* are quiet-water free swimmers, and some, such as *Isonychia,* are fast-water free swimmers.

Most types of mayflies actually must have their particular type of water to survive. It is evident that a river with most or all of the different environments will have a larger variety of species than a fast, rocky stream with no weed beds, no mudbanks, or quiet waters. The latter stream would be lacking entire families of mayflies and this would reduce the variety of hatches considerably. A fly-fisherman who likes to cast over rising trout would obviously be much better off choosing a river with a variety of water-bottom types.

CHAPTER 5

Patterns Evolved— No-Hackle Duns, Paraduns, Emerging Patterns, Spinners

VARIOUS ARTIFICIALS COMING INTO THE WINDOW

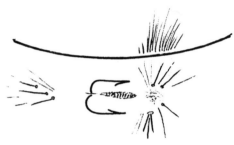

Standard hackle fly

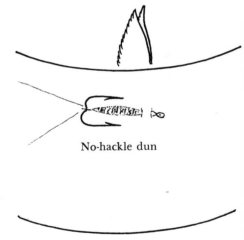

No-hackle dun

EXAMINATION OF INITIAL photographic efforts substantiated our original feeling concerning the need for improved patterns. Countless failures with "standard" dressings had built up a tremendous desire for alteration and improvement. Our initial photographs may have been lacking in clarity and quality, but they certainly were good enough to get us started in the right direction. No more than a casual glance was required to spin the wheels of creativity. It became obvious that we had confronted ourselves with a new concept, a fresh approach, and likewise a distinct challenge.

Probably the most exciting aspect was the challenge of devising and constructing imitations based on our careful observation and interpretation of the photomacrographs. As most flytiers know, there is nothing more satisfying than to contrive a new idea for a fly, assemble it at the bench, and then discover that it achieves at least some degree of success in the stream. Such auspicious episodes, however, usually expand one's ego but generally overestimate the actual effectiveness of the imitation. It is satisfying to concoct a new pattern and doggedly declare it to be the best and only pattern that you will cast upon the water, but pursuit of this

Hen spinner not yet in window

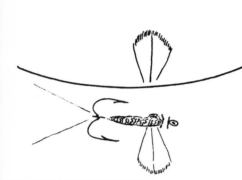

Hen spinner with one wing in film and out of window—other wing slightly off surface of water and in window

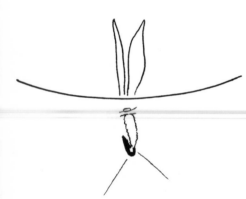

Front view of no-hackle dun coming into window

Paradun coming into window

procedure is neither sensible nor productive. Unfortunately, most flies designed in this manner are merely created in accordance to the whims and fancies of the flytier. Assuredly, these creations will be effective in taking fish *part* of the time, but let's be realistic: there are times when almost *anything* will work. These are the "easy" periods when trout can be taken without much effort or difficulty. *Everyone* should be experiencing action during this time of low selectivity. Such periods should scarcely be ignored or thought of as offering little or no sport; on the contrary, it's always a pleasure to be in the stream and doing "business," no matter what degree of angling difficulty prevails. In fact, these are probably the best periods for the neophyte to get acclimated to the sport and to catch a few fish; they will certainly whet his interest. In addition, the expert can sharpen his casting, work on new techniques, test the durability and floatability of new flies, and also increase his score in the process.

The real challenge, however, comes when the trout become *selective*. Steady feeders that zero-in on a certain fly can be extremely difficult to fool, especially with some of the "shaving brush" patterns that probably look like gigantic monstrosities to the fish. Close-up views of these unnatural looking bristlelike artificials must make the trout wonder what strange new creature is invading his domain.

Many of the standard patterns are so ridiculous that we fishermen, thirty feet away, could easily see our artificial stand out like a sore thumb as it drifted with a group of naturals. Most of you have no doubt had this experience. But *stop and think:* if *you* can tell the difference thirty feet away, the trout three inches away must be having hysterics. At any rate, he can be very reluctant to take our offering unless it is a fairly accurate simulation of the real thing. Thus, when the fish become highly selective, we must make every effort to reproduce the outstanding features of the natural. This includes not only characteristics of size, shape, and color, but also such peculiarities as how the fly floats on the water and how it behaves in its environment.

Probably the most important aspect of our approach in developing new patterns was maintaining an open mind. We more or less had to pretend that standard dressings and techniques never existed, so that our thinking would not be influenced or affected by precedent or habit. Usually, a routine method of action or procedure is very difficult to change. Human nature seems to dictate that we follow the path of least resistance and, unfortunately, this is the route of passive conformity. Today, in many fields of endeavor, traditional ideas are being challenged, changed, and modified in order to bring about progress. Likewise, in this modern era of super-selective trout and heavily fished streams, we must keep an open and inquiring mind if we hope to create the patterns needed for selective situations. The lore and heritage of our "sport of sports" are vital to the complete enjoyment and appreciation of fly-fishing; but true inventiveness and originality are also part of the fly-fisherman's heritage—for many patterns that are now considered "traditional" were once dramatic innovations themselves. Since traditional patterns are not always effective during periods of high selectivity, we must be willing to deviate from the path of conformity and pursue a fresh approach.

Ideas for new patterns resulted mainly from the observation of our color photographs. Depending on the size of the insect, most of these pictures, or photomacrographs, were shot anywhere from one to four times life size. Probably the greatest majority, flies that ranged from five to ten millimeters in length, were taken at magnifications between 2X and 3X. The main object was to fill the viewing area of the lens as much as possible without cutting off any of the important features. This procedure provided pictures that permitted detailed study of the characteristics of each species. Critical features such as size, shape, proportion, and color could thus easily be observed and examined.

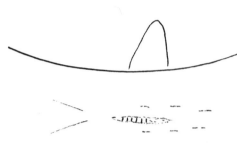

Natural approaching window —only abdomen, tails, and part of legs visible

Colors as seen under these magnifications are the ones the trout seem to prefer. Many naturals appear to be one color when held in the hand or seen floating *on* the water, but when viewed under magnification are another color entirely. We have experimented many times using both colors and have found that the artificial utilizing the color revealed in our photographs is normally much more effective. This was vividly illustrated in our search for a better *Ephemerella dorothea* imitation. The standard yellow-bodied pattern worked well on occasion, but was not consistent. Naked-eye observation of hand-held specimens indicated the validity of this dressing, but examination of magnified color pictures revealed the presence of either an orange or olive cast, depending on locality. Addition of either the orange or olive element to the pattern has increased its effectiveness tremendously. Another example of this color phenomenon concerns certain members of the Baetidae family. Many of these minute species are more popularly known as Blue-winged Olives, supposedly because they exhibit wings that appear blue and bodies that appear olive in color. However, under magnification, some of these "olive" bodies surprisingly turn out to be brownish and the wings more grayish than blue.

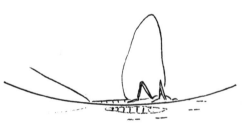

first glimpse of wing in window

Proper shape and proportion are extremely important in the construction of effective patterns. Most mayfly duns and spinners have slender delicate bodies and imitations should be dressed accordingly; few current artificials exhibit this quality, though. Nymphal bodies, on the other hand, are generally more varied in shape and can be round, flat, oval, slender, or robust. These exact shapes and proportions can easily be determined from close examination of our photographs. This information can then be applied in the tying process to produce more realistic flies. Body silhouette is probably more critical in the construction of nymphs than dry flies, mainly because the body is the most outstanding feature of the nymph.

body half in, half out of window

In considering the dry fly, however, we must be equally concerned with the shape of *both* body and wings. When the freshly hatched dun approaches the "window," the first elements to be seen *clearly* and *completely* by the trout are the wings. This visual contact is important, as the rise is initiated or triggered at this time. The wings of our artificial must provide a close representation of the wings of the natural so the trout will respond and begin the rise. The body, however, is just as important. Even though the

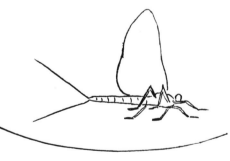

Mayfly completely in window

wings have been accepted and the rise has been triggered, the final decision as to the authenticity of the offering has yet to be made. At this point, before contact is accomplished, the entire fly enters the window, allowing close examination by the trout. During this final critical observation both wings and body must be right or a refusal will result. This reasoning can be used to explain the so-called short strikes we often encounter and also those times when the trout come up, look at our fly, and then drop back into their feeding position.

One of the more difficult problems of fly tying is to procure suitable wing materials that will hold their shape when wet. More research is required in this critical area but, for the present, some of the better wing materials include duck-shoulder feathers, turkey-body feathers, shaped hackles, hackle fibers, and various types of hair. Legs and tails normally show up very little in most species and can hardly be considered as outstanding physical features. The tails of the artificial fly, however, have an extremely important function in the positioning of the fly on the water. Stiff high-quality fibers should be utilized and then spread, or split, at a wide angle. Fibers attached in this manner form outriggers, or stabilizers, that keep the fly in an upright position. This position is absolutely necessary for the effective simulation of a newly hatched dun. Hackle or hackle fibers can be used to represent legs but they are not necessary for this purpose. Depending on individual preference, hackle may be used for flotation but should be kept as sparse as possible. Actually, if proper materials and techniques are used, hackle is not normally required.

The single most important discovery we made for dry flies, which we cannot emphasize enough, is that *flies tied with spun-fur bodies on 3X fine-wire hooks need no hackle to float them.* In fact, when properly treated with floatant, it is almost impossible to sink them when you try.*

One of the most essential yet seemingly simple aspects of creating a deadly pattern is size. This is especially true for the smaller flies, less than seven or eight millimeters in length. If, for example, we are trying to imitate a natural that is five millimeters long and our artificial ends up being six millimeters long, we are a whopping 20 percent too large. One millimeter doesn't sound like much, but it can mean the difference between success and failure, particularly when diminutive patterns are employed. The best procedure is to measure the natural accurately and then tie the artificial on a hook bearing a shank of the proper length. At streamside, it is best to utilize a small hand magnifier in obtaining an accurate comparison of artificial to natural. This identification part of our study requires precise measurement of each specimen and this information is then put to use in the tying process. It is far better to use actual measurements when describing patterns rather than hook size. Hook specifications differ greatly and are therefore unreliable for our purpose other than as a general denotation of size.

Another factor that affected the development of new patterns was the

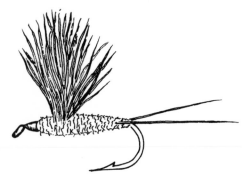

Duck-quill segment clump
no-hackle

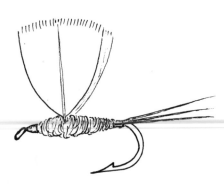

Duck-shoulder no-hackle

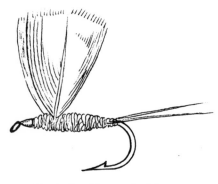

Duck-shoulder no-hackle

* We recently learned of a new and extraordinarily good body material, Polypropylene. It floats extremely well (specific gravity approximately .94) and is strong, durable, and realistic in appearance. Phentex is the trade name of this yarn; it is distributed by Pic Corporation, 32 Main Street, Norwalk, Connecticut.

action, or lack of action, of each species, both in, on, and above the water. Most of this information was gained through observations made at streamside or at the aquarium. The majority of in-water activity was observed in the home aquariums, where nymphal life could easily be inspected on a day-to-day basis. Watching the nymphs move about and emerge into adults provided valuable knowledge for designing new subsurface and in-the-film patterns. Streamside observations furnished criteria for new adult dressings and corresponding techniques for their effective application.

What specific patterns evolved from our study? They are divided into four classifications: nymphs, duns, spinners, and downwings. Since the major portion of our work dealt with Ephemeroptera, the first three categories are concerned only with mayfly patterns, while dressings for some of the other insects will be covered under Downwings.

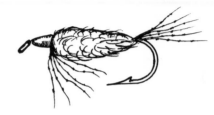

NYMPHS

Probably the most basic requirement of a nymphal pattern is that some type of fur should be used for the body. Other materials such as quills, floss, wool, thread, and plastics may look enticing in the vise, but they take on a distinctly unnatural appearance when wet. Our nymphs have bodies constructed from such furs as rabbit, muskrat, opossum, fox, mole, and beaver. Fine-textured furs should be utilized for small flies, size #20 and under—not only for appearance but also for ease of spinning. White domestic rabbit is an excellent dubbing material because it can be readily dyed to the proper color and it is usually fine grained. Tails from wild rabbits have the added advantage of providing many light to dark shades when dyed a certain color. Legs and tails are normally best imitated with such feathers as wood duck, mallard, or partridge tinted to the proper shade. Some of the better wing-case materials include ostrich herl, quill segments, breast feathers, and fur.

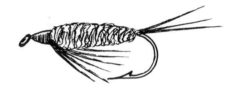

Various nymphs tied without a wing case

An all-fur nymph, #16

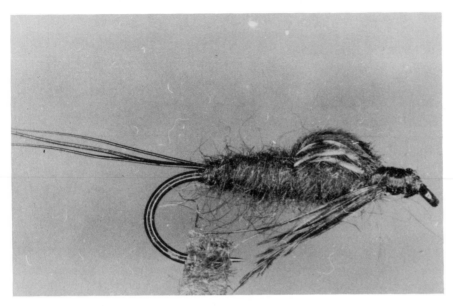

Dorothea nymph, #16

Hendrickson nymph, #14

Ostrich herl nymphs

Fur case nymphs

Extended-body nymphs, with quill segment cases

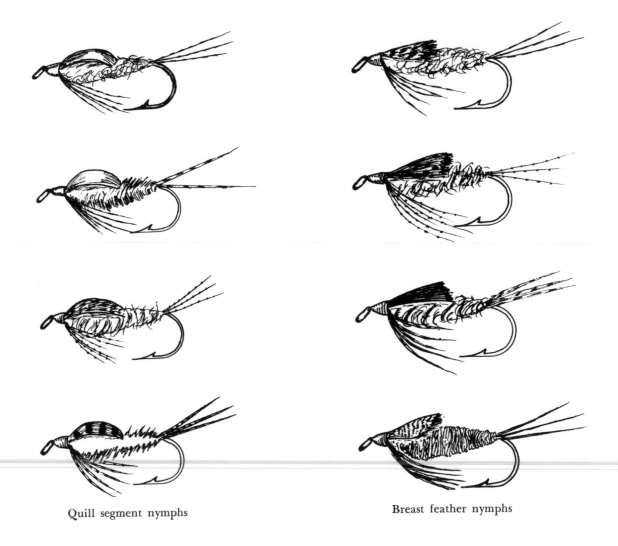

Quill segment nymphs

Breast feather nymphs

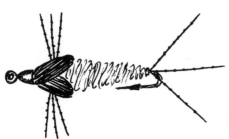

Quill segment case, crisscrossed;
legs extending from sides; tails split

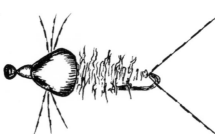

Quill segment case; legs extended
from sides; fur picked to simulate
gills; tails split

Breast feather case; legs tied on
sides but swept back; tails split

HOW TO TIE AN
EXTENDED-BODY
WIGGLE NYMPH

1. Make a loop from a thin strand of piano wire, the length you desire for the abdomen of the nymph

Observation of nymphs swimming about in the aquarium revealed possibilities for several different patterns. We noticed that many species, especially *Ephemerella, Stenonema,* and *Leptophlebia,* swim with a distinct undulating movement of the abdomen. Also, the front pair of legs extends forward while the middle and hind pair extend to the rear. Attempts to imitate this situation resulted in extended-body and "wiggle" nymphs.

The extended-body nymph has the abdomen tied on a piece of wire that can be bent in any direction. This makes the nymph look more realistic and is simple to tie. The wiggle nymph, however, carries the idea a step further by adding a hinge between the thorax and abdomen. This allows the rear part of the fly to move freely and more closely simulate the movement of the real nymph. The wiggle nymph is somewhat more difficult to tie but, like anything else, can be mastered with a little practice. Many methods can be used, but probably the best utilizes very fine wire for the hinge. Use a short-shank hook for the thorax and leave a small loop of wire extended from the bend. Loop another piece of wire through the first loop and then construct the abdomen and tails on the doubled-back piece. An easier method is to tie the back part of the fly on a small hook first, and then cut off the bend. Attach this part (the abdomen) to the thorax with a fine wire or monofilament loop. We've also used rubber bands and plain tying thread for the hinge. As for the legs, let most of the fibers extend backward conventionally, but tie a few of them forward. Sometimes stiffer materials, such as deer hair or porcupine, are necessary for the front legs. These extended-body and wiggle nymphs have proved themselves to be very effective, not only in matching the hatch, but when used as attractors.

2. Put the loop in a fly-tying vise and tie on tails and fur body so just the loop sticks out from the body

3. Make another loop of piano wire and insert in the first loop; the abdomen is tied on through the second loop to form a hinge. Then tie the second hinge on top of a 5X short shank hook

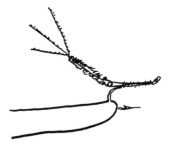

4. Tie thorax, wing cases, and hackle on the hook part of the nymph and finish as usual

Pale Morning Dun emerger, duck-quill segment type, #18

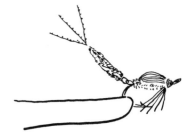

An emerger, tied with hackle points, #16

Wiggle nymph with breast feather case (arrow and dotted lines illustrate action)

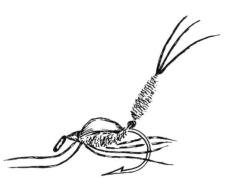

Wiggle nymph with quill segment case; front legs tied forward

Imitations of the emerging nymph are probably the most deadly and effective patterns of all, and many fish are fooled throughout the season by this breed of artificial. Numerous reasons can be cited to explain the effectiveness of the emerging pattern. When tied with short wings and on heavy hooks, it is an excellent nymphal imitation that can be fished deep. When tied on medium-weight hooks and dressed with longer wings, it is deadly during the initial stages of the hatch. On fine wire hooks, it can often be fished very effectively through the entire hatch. In fact, it can be treated with a floatant and will often produce more strikes than the subimago imitation. In general, emerging patterns are identical to standard nymphal patterns, except that wings replace wing cases. Hackle points do a good job of simulating the newly sprouted wings, but duck-shoulder feathers, hackle fibers, hair, fur, and shaped feathers are also recommended.

DUNS

Our imitations of freshly hatched subimagos are tied with materials and techniques similar to those used for nymphal patterns—with a few exceptions. Tails, for example, should be fashioned from stiff, top-quality hackle fibers and spread as far as possible. As mentioned before, it is very important to follow this procedure to ensure proper positioning of the fly on the water. Stiff fibers spread in this manner act as stabilizers to keep the fly in an upright position. Legs, when imitated, should likewise be constructed of top quality hackle since this will provide better flotation than the breast or body feathers used in nymphal construction. The use of fur for dun bodies affords the same advantages obtained in the underwater dressings; it also floats beautifully when treated with dry-fly solution. Next

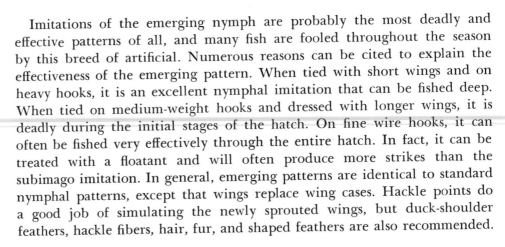

to fur, some of the synthetic yarns, due to their low moisture absorption and color availability, can be fabricated into attractive high-floating bodies. To date, however, most of these materials are a little too coarse to provide the slender delicate bodies needed on sizes #22 and smaller. Various quills certainly make good-looking bodies, but contrary to popular opinion, most do not float too well. Furs such as muskrat, opossum, mole, fitch, rabbit, and beaver, when treated with a floatant, are vastly superior to any other material we know of at the present time. They are available in a variety of colors, are easy to work with, are durable, and look realistic on the finished fly.

The greatest variable found in the construction of the floating dun undoubtedly lies in wing construction, both in materials and techniques. Materials include hackle points, shaped feathers, breast and body feathers, hair, fur, and hackle fibers, and they can be altered and varied utilizing many methods. One very effective type is the shaped wing, which is usually made from the webby section of a hackle, a body feather, or a small duck-wing-shoulder feather. They are cut out with scissors or a razor blade to the exact size and shape of the species being imitated. Used singly or in pairs, these wings are very deadly, but must be shaped and mounted very carefully to prevent leader twist. The addition of lacquer or cement to these wings adds not only to the appearance and durability, but also eliminates wing shrinkage when the fly gets wet in use.

Parachute patterns have been very effective when duns are on the water, probably because this type of fly can hardly help but land right side up, every cast. We have used parachutes for a long time to imitate the large Ephemeridae duns, but had never tried them for small flies. Initial attempts with #18s and #20s were successful, and now we tie them all the way down to #28s. The hackle is mainly to position the fly properly on the

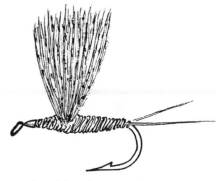

Partridge clump no-hackle

Paradun—shaped hen-hackle fiber type, #18

Paradun, #16—photographed
from underwater

Paradun with hen hackle fibers

Extended-body paradun—elk wings, deer-hair body

VARIOUS WING MATERIALS

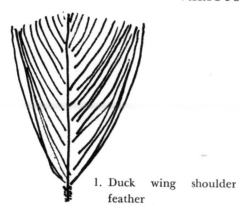

1. Duck wing shoulder feather

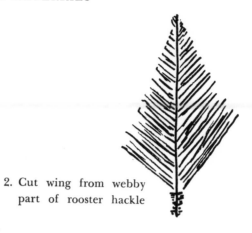

2. Cut wing from webby part of rooster hackle

3. Hen hackle tip

4. Clump of hen hackle fibers

5. Clump of elk hair

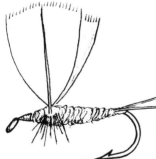

Duck shoulder "V" hackle

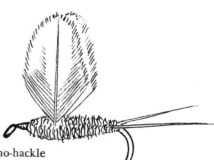

Hen-hackle tip no-hackle

HOW TO PREPARE A SHAPED WING FROM THE WEBBY PART OF A ROOSTER HACKLE

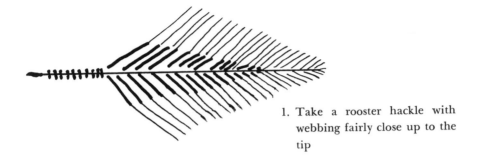

1. Take a rooster hackle with webbing fairly close up to the tip

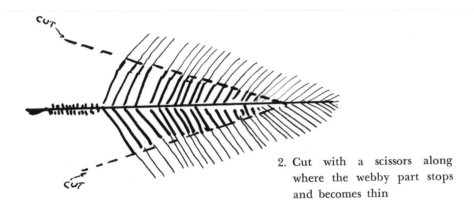

2. Cut with a scissors along where the webby part stops and becomes thin

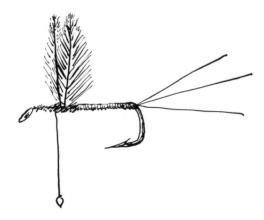

3. Make a pair of these and tie in as an upright divided wing

water; it is *not* for flotation, and should be kept as sparse as possible. Hackle that is too heavy will only obscure the delicate outline so necessary for success with these small patterns. Hair, shaped feathers, and hackle fibers can all be used to make excellent wings for these flies.

The most deadly pattern to evolve from our study is the no-hackle fly. Observation of our photographic efforts indicated that legs play a very insignificant role in the outline of most mayflies. This fact prompted a close-up study of standard artificials, where we noticed that *hackle was a ridiculous imitation of legs*. It was not only too bushy, but also obscured the outline of both body and wings. Instead of being the least significant feature, as it should have been, it was by far the *most* significant feature. The obvious solution was to cut down or eliminate the hackle altogether. This we did, and when combined with fur bodies, split tails, and various wings, the new no-hackle flies produced results far superior to those of any flies we had ever tried.

The most important point to remember when tying no-hackle flies is to spread the tail fibers as much as possible in a horizontal plane. This will ensure proper position on the water and guarantee upright wings. Excellent flotation will be assured if light wire hooks and dubbed bodies are utilized.

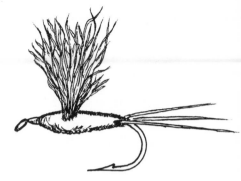

Hair clump no-hackle

A standard Western Green Drake, #10, from underwater

A standard Pale Evening Dun, #18, from underwater

No-hackle dun, duck-shoulder wings, #16—photographed from underwater

No-hackle dun—duck-quill segment type, #16

No-hackle dun, duck-quill segment type, #16, from underwater

No-hackle with wings
mounted on sides—
gray/yellow, duck-quill
segment type

Another no-hackle with
wings mounted slightly
differently on sides

No-hackle dun,
duck-shoulder type, #12

No-hackle with "V"-style
duck-quill segment wings
mounted on sides

Actually, no-hackle flies are very simple to tie, making the imitation of small naturals extremely simple. Even the neophyte flytier will experience little difficulty in constructing artificials on the smallest hooks.

The use of turkey-body feathers has contributed greatly to the minute no-hackle flies. Originally on size #22 hooks, and smaller, we employed stripped hackle fibers tied on in a clump for wings. This required trimming with a pair of scissors, which, in turn, left a rather unappealing wing outline. Natural tips are much more desirable and can be obtained by using the square-tipped turkey feathers. Another advantage of the turkey feathers is that they are white and can therefore be dyed to the desired color. They handle very well and are also very durable.

SPINNERS

Three types of spinners have proven extremely effective for us; all are no-hackle flies except for some of the larger imitations, size #10 and up. The first is tied with hen hackle-feather tips; these are wide and webby and, when tied spent, present a beautiful wing outline, lying flush in the water. When preparing these feathers, it is important to trim the excess fibers with the scissors or to leave them whole. If the excess fibers are stripped, the quill is weakened, creating a condition that normally results in a poor wing silhouette. It is also advisable to point the wings slightly forward to compensate for current and casting forces.

The second type of spinner employs light partridge-breast feathers tied spent or half spent; it is deadly during the *Ephemerella dorothea* spinner fall. These feathers, when wet, not only become quite transparent, but also their speckled appearance simulates the venation of the naturals. The easiest method of assembly is to tie them on in a clump and figure-eight them into two equal sections. Both the partridge and hen-hackle spinners must be well soaked in dry-fly floatant. Other body, breast, and shoulder feathers have also proved successful for this type of fly.

Large extended-body
hen spinner, #8

Hen spinner, #18

Hen spinner, #16,
from underwater

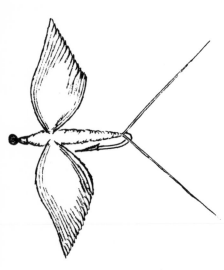

Duck-quill segment spinner

The third spinner type is simple to tie and is constructed of wound hackle. Spinners with their wings upright can be represented with fully wound hackle, while intermediate- to full-spent positions can be represented by trimming to shape. Another method of obtaining these positions is to put the dubbing on last and figure-eight the hackle fibers into position. Depending on the species being imitated, the most effective colors are light-blue dun, medium-blue dun, and bronze-blue dun. In some cases, the addition of one or two turns of grizzly increases the effectiveness greatly. Also, a more realistic and durable wing outline can be maintained if a very fine tying thread is wound through the hackle. This procedure acts to stiffen and flare the fibers.

Effective imitation of the larger flies, in sizes #4 to #10, is accomplished with hen-hackle tips accompanied by sparse, undersize hackle. Both hackle and hackle tips should blend together to form the general color of the wing; on some of the large flies, such as *Hexagenia*, double wings can be used, putting grizzly on top and blue dun on the bottom. With this combination, the grizzly represents the dark splotches in the venation, while blue dun represents the general coloration on the water. The grizzly tips can be seen through the blue dun but are toned down to a more realistic shade.

In general, light hooks and dubbed bodies should be utilized to provide proper flotation, and tails should be long, stiff fibered, and spread. For the larger flies, however, excellent bodies, either regular or extended, can be fashioned from materials such as deer-body hair and some of the new synthetic yarns. Tails should be spread not for mechanical reasons, as they are for the no-hackle duns, but because they add greatly to the realistic appearance of the artificial.

DOWNWINGS

The materials and techniques required for caddis-fly, stone-fly, and midge imitations are basically identical to those used for the upwings. The bodies of all stages—nymph, pupa, and adult, for example—are mainly constructed of fur. Wing cases are made of ostrich herl, quill segments, fur, and shoulder feathers. Wings are fashioned from hen-hackle feathers, duck quill, partridge, hair, and hackle fibers. Probably the major difference is the use of more hackle in simulating flying or skittering adults.

Our caddis-fly imitations are divided into three types: pupas, adults at rest, and flying adults. A simple yet deadly pupa pattern for size #20 and smaller consists merely of a fur body and either a collar or beard made of partridge. The most common body colors are green, tan, and gray. For size #18 and larger, wing pads and a fuzzy, shaggy head can be added. The wing pads are best simulated with duck-shoulder feathers or quill segments. Dark gray to black are the most common colors. These feathers should be placed in a low position on each side of the body. The pupal head is made by forming a small clump of dark gray fur just behind the eye of the hook: this fur should then be picked with a dubbing needle to create a shaggy texture.

1—UPRIGHT	2—UPRIGHT	3—HALF SPENT	4—FULL SPENT	5—WET
FULLY HACKLED — FLOAT HIGH ON SURFACE	HACKLED, CLIPPED ON BOTTOM ONLY — LOWER FLOAT	HACKLE CLIPPED TO "V" POSITION — LOW FLOAT	HEN, PARTRIDGE OR TRIMMED HACKLE — WINGS FLUSH	HEAVY WIRE — HEN WINGS — FISH WET

SWARMING, MATING AND FALL TO SURFACE

EGGS

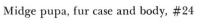

SPINNER SEQUENCE AND POSSIBLE PATTERNS

Midge pupa, fur case and body, #24

Caddis pupa, #16

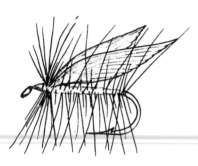

Flying caddis with duck-quill
segment wings, palmer hackle

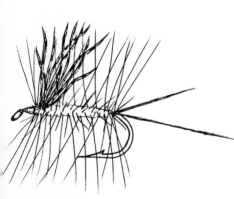

Flying caddis with partridge
clump wings, palmer hackle

One of the most effective and exacting imitations of an adult caddis at
rest is a fat, fur body with a pair of wide, webby, hen hackles tied flat. If
hackle is desired, add sparse blue dun or grizzly tied Palmer, clipped top
and bottom. An even more realistic version is to wind the hackle on only
the front one-third of the body. Other materials that make excellent wings
for this type of fly include duck-quill segments, partridge, and hen-hackle
fibers. The duck-quill-segment type looks more like a real caddis fly, if the
wings are put on separately with concave sides down and tips to the outside.
A more generalized, but very effective, pattern is one that utilizes groundhog
hair for the wings. This type of artificial is recommended for unknown or
strange water situations.

The most common imitation of a flying caddis is the Adams-type fly. Just
vary the body and wing coloration to suit the natural. A selection of these
flies with green, tan, and gray bodies tied in sizes #16 through #20 will
cover most flying-caddis situations. Both of the other types used to simulate
flying or skittering caddis are Palmer hackle flies. One consists of only a fur
body and Palmer hackle, while the other has a pair of duck-quill wings
added, before the hackle is wound. If quality hackle and light hooks are
used, these flies float high and are easy to skitter and skip over the water.

Most midge patterns are tied on the smallest of hooks, #24 and #28,
and we find that these minute imitations are much more effective if kept
simple and uncomplicated. Either an all-fur body or a combination thread-
and-fur body is all that's required for the pupal imitation. The abdomen,
whether fashioned from fur or thread, should be very slim, while the thorax
should be more robust and made of fur. Small wing pads made from quill
segments or shoulder feathers can be added over the thorax if a more detailed pattern is desired. Olive and brownish olive are the most common
body colors and wing pads are blackish.

Adult midges are best imitated with a slim fur body and wings of either hen-hackle tips or duck-quill segments tied flat over the body. Partridge may also be used effectively as a wing material.

Flying adults can be simulated with tiny hackle flies, tied regular or Palmer style. Probably our most effective pattern has blue dun tails, a dark mole body, and slightly oversized hackle—dark blue dun and grizzly mixed. This fly rides high on the water and imitates the skittering adult.

With the exception of double wing cases, stone-fly nymphs are tied with materials and techniques identical to those used for mayflies. Quite often the fur bodies are weighted with lead to facilitate the bottom bumping that is sometimes required with these patterns. For nymphal imitations, size #12 and larger, goose- or condor-quill fibers are more realistic than partridge for tails and legs. We prefer quill segments and ostrich clumps for the double wing cases.

Groundhog hair, because of its variegated coloration, is an excellent wing material for imitating adult stone flies at rest. Hen-hackle tips and duck-quill segments are also good, especially on the smaller sizes, #14 and under. Flying stones require Adams or Palmer type artificials, similar to those used for flying caddis. In all cases, try to match the wing and body coloration of the naturals as closely as possible.

Midge pupa, fur case,
quill body, #24

Hen caddis,
palmer hackle, #18

Midge pupa, fur case,
quill body, #24

Caddis—shaped wings,
palmer hackle, #16

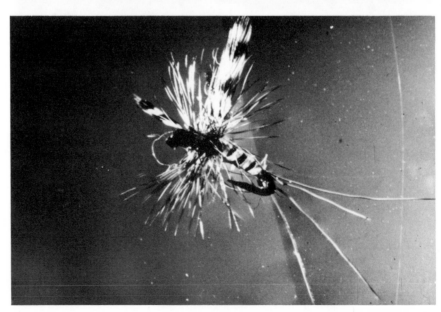

Mosquito, or Adams-type,
#18, from underwater

CHAPTER 6

Streamside Procedure

THE CARDINAL RULE of streamside procedure is "Get a Sample." No matter how well we are acquainted with a stream and its hatches, it is imperative that specimens be caught and examined closely on every trip. General observation of a natural as it floats by or flies overhead is not sufficient. Specimens must be captured and held at close range so that color and size can be determined. A small and inexpensive hand magnifier should be carried at all times to facilitate these investigations. It is also advisable to put some of the naturals in small containers and save them for further inspection. Actually, close-up observation requires very little time and effort, but is extremely important to successful hatch-matching. Many species, for example, appear to be a certain color and size when viewed from a distance, but take on a different appearance at close range. The trout does his viewing with the naturals floating right in front of his nose, so it makes sense that the angler follow the same procedure. The most critical characteristics of the natural are body color, wing color, and size. Armed with this information, we can select the proper artificial from the supply at hand or utilize a streamside tying kit to fashion the desired combination of fur and feathers.

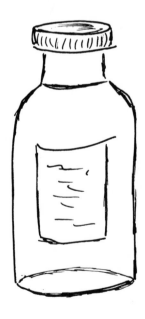

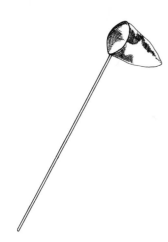

Long-handled butterfly
net, 8 feet long

When fishing in strange water or in water where the hatch is unpredictable, definite preliminary steps should be taken. The first is to fight the natural urge to get geared up and into the water as fast as possible. Those who jump out of the car, rush into the stream, and start beating the water with what worked well two weeks before, or last year or for a friend on some other river at another time, will usually get skunked. It's far better to slow down and perform a little basic research that will provide a great deal of valuable information. The benefits of pursuing this course of action will certainly outweigh the small amount of lost fishing time. Some type of hand net or seine should be a standard item carried in the trunk of the car. An inexpensive kitchen strainer attached to a wooden handle or bamboo pole is adequate. Nymphs can easily be seined with such a device by kicking the stream bottom and holding the strainer downstream. Captured specimens can be used for identification of the upcoming hatch and also as tying models for effective nymphal and emerging patterns. Here again, the hand magnifier is invaluable for close-up observation. Seining should be performed in various places to get a good cross-sectional look at the total life in the stream. Riffles, runs, silt beds, backwaters, eddies, and weed beds should all be investigated. Items such as logs, sticks, leaves, stones, and plant life can be picked up by hand and studied closely for nymphal life.*

Molting spinners afford a greater challenge, but can usually be located with a little perseverance. Some species seem to prefer certain kinds of trees or bushes for their final molt, while others can be found on such objects as bridge abutments, cabin walls, light fixtures, and screen doors. Dead spinners from the previous day can be located in quiet backwaters on logs, snags, and weed beds or found entangled in webs spun by spiders and insect larvae. The capture of airborne spinners from the mating flight is best accomplished with a long-handled butterfly net, though, if the angler is quick of hand, he can usually snare a few low-flying specimens.

Now that our initial research has been accomplished by seining for nymphs and checking for spinners, it is time to assemble the rod and do some fishing. Let's assume that there is a distinct lack of feeding or hatch activity on the stream. Probably the best bet would be to tie on a nymphal pattern that imitates the most predominant specimen found during the seining process or the one that appears to be ready for emergence. Nymphs that are close to hatching usually display darkened wing cases and are active. Sometimes a light line can be seen on the covert where the outer skin is starting to split. Try to match the size, shape, and color of the natural as closely as possible. Remember, it's the color and appearance of the artificial when it's *wet* that is important. Always moisten the fly in your mouth or in the stream to get the proper effect.

Try various casting, floating, and retrieving techniques with your nymph to see which is most effective. The typical quartering upstream, dead-drift technique is not always the best. Try various combinations of casting angles coupled with floats that range from dead drift to an erratic pulsating action. Fishing the nymph directly upstream can be very effective, but long fine

Long-handled seine,
5 feet long

* Seining nymphs is illegal in some states; check local regulations.

leaders and delicate casting are essential. Downstream nymphing is especially deadly on certain hatches, but it must be combined with well-executed lazy S and curve casts.

Often the long upstream cast, followed first by a slow sinking action and then by an accelerated escape-to-the-surface movement, is the most productive technique. Occasionally, a downstream cast, followed by a fast erratic retrieve, will produce strikes when all else fails. The main thing to remember when nymphing in unfamiliar waters is to *be creative*. Investigate to find out what forms of underwater life are present and then experiment with various techniques of presenting a suitable imitation.

Wiggle nymph with quill segment case

Nymphal imitations are normally fished until emergence time, and then, for many species, it is best to switch to an emerging pattern. This type of fly is similar to the nymph, except that wings are replaced with wing cases. These patterns are more or less a combination of nymph and dun features, and can be fished under, in, or on the surface film. Thus, the emerging pattern is a highly versatile fly that can be used effectively during several phases of the hatch. As a result, these flies should be tied on both heavy- and light-wire hooks, and some of the light-wire variety should be soaked in dry-fly floatant. Most nymphs split out of their cases at the surface and struggle a bit as they float along. To simulate this activity, an emerging pattern tied on a light hook should be drifted through rising trout with an occasional twitch. Some nymphs, however, uncase their wings underwater and swim to the surface in the dun form. Simulation of this habit is accomplished by sinking a heavy-wire pattern and then rising it in front of a feeding fish. The emerging fly is most deadly right at the beginning of the hatch. This is the period when the fish are just beginning to take a few duns on the surface, but are still taking most of their food slightly under or in the film. They have become conscious of wings emerging into view but are reluctant to feed steadily on the surface. The sight of emergent wings seems to excite the trout into frenzied feeding activity and solid strikes. Even after most of the fish have commenced steady surface feeding, the emerging pattern can be very effective. A light-wire version, soaked in floatant and then drifted along on the surface, is sometimes more deadly than a delicate high-floating dun pattern.

As the hatch progresses, a moment is usually reached when most of the trout become partial to duns only. They know exactly what they want and become very selective. This is the beginning of great frustration for many fishermen, when actually it should be the period when the greatest harvest is reaped. This is the time when the trout is most vulnerable *if* the angler has the *right fly* and knows how to use it. Repeated failures during these situations can drive a good man crazy, but there's no need for such anxiety if a little common sense is applied. First, determine what insect the trout are feeding on and then get a sample of it. Sometimes, determining which fly is being taken can be a problem, but if you really put your nose down into the water and observe closely, the situation can usually be resolved. If necessary, wade right into the main line of drift even if it means spooking a few fish; they'll normally return to their feeding stations within a minute or two after you leave anyway. Once you've determined what the fish are

Wiggle nymph with fur case

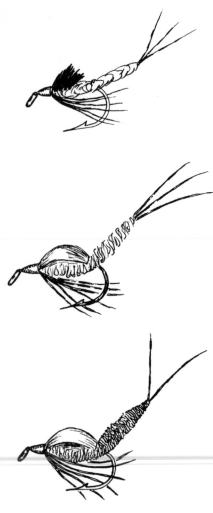

Extended-body nymphs—1 ostrich clump and 2 segment
cases

feeding on, catch a specimen, even though you're positive you know the species; a small aquarium hand net should be carried to facilitate this process. Determine the body color, wing color, and exact size of the fly. Color can be interpreted only by each individual, but size should be accurately measured, preferably with a millimeter gauge. Size cannot be overemphasized as an extremely important hatch-matching characteristic, especially on the smaller sizes. As mentioned earlier, an error of only one millimeter can make an enormous difference between natural and artificial. The average mayfly is only about 7 mm in length, which would be a size #16, so if your imitation is one or two millimeters too long on what should be a small or average-size fly, it will look enormous to the trout (see Appendix B). No matter how perfect the imitation, it will never fool a selective riser if it has unrealistic dimensions.

With the required color and size in mind, select a fly that you think will do the job. If a suitable imitation cannot be found, sometimes another fly can be trimmed or manicured. The final alternative is to utilize a portable fly-tying kit, which should be standard equipment in one's fishing gear. It certainly is difficult to leave rising trout, but if you are stranded without the right pattern, it is better to sacrifice a little fishing time and spend a few profitable minutes at the vise. Besides simulating color and size as closely as possbile, it is important to tie a fly that will land upright and present a good wing outline. The outstanding feature of the freshly emerged dun is the wing silhouette, which creates a sailboatlike appearance. This feature must be imitated in the artificial. Once the right pattern has been fashioned, it should be fished with or without movement, depending on the behavior of the drifting dun.

The fall of a spinner flight can provide fantastic fishing for the initiated and much vexation for the neophyte. An angler who is prepared with the right pattern—and who can determine when to use it—will enjoy some of the finest fishing available. However, the uninitiated usually experience great difficulty in determining what the trout are feeding on during these periods. This problem is due mainly to the fact that imagos, especially the spent-wing variety, are very hard to see in the water. A hatch of duns is quite obvious because the upright wings are opaque and easy to see, but spinners, even as large as Hendricksons, can be very difficult to perceive because of the clear wings and low-floating body position. They can be seen in the air before the fall takes place, but if a fisherman is not oriented to this habit, they can easily go undetected. Many anglers concentrate so hard on their fly that they are completely unaware of any activity around them. Also, the spinners of some species seem to prefer certain riffles and runs and could, therefore, fall upstream and go unnoticed.

The best procedure for detecting spinners is to stay as alert as possible. Look up frequently to see if flights are forming. On a bright day, even high-flying spinners can be spotted as their wings glisten in the sun. Another excellent indicator is to watch the birds. When spinners are in the air, birds become very active and dive into the swarm to get an easy meal. Once the spinners are on the water, close observation may be required to see them. Always get a sample with the hand net and examine it for color and size. Patterns are simple to tie, consisting of tails, dubbed bodies, and hackle or hackle points for the wing. When hackle is used, it is left full or trimmed to various angulations, depending on the wing position of the natural. Flotation is a problem with the full-spent patterns, so extrafine wire hooks are a must.

The portable streamside tying kit is essential to successful fishing and rare is the trip when we do not utilize ours. It need not be fancy or large, but should be made up of a minimum number of basic tools and materials. The ideal vise should be mounted on a pedestal so that it can be used anywhere. Other tools are standard and include scissors, hackle pliers, dubbing needle, razor blades, and tweezers. Most flies can be made from two materials, fur and hackle, so a small box of fur in assorted colors and several necks form the staple of the kit. Besides hooks and thread, other important items include woodduck, duck shoulder, turkey, and partridge.

Keeping a diary or some other form of written notes concerning each trip is another important phase of streamside procedure. The accumulation of this information can be invaluable, and the more of it that is collected the greater chance you will have for successful fishing in the future. Since most hatches occur at approximately the same time every year on the same stream, the recording of this knowledge can be used year after year as an accurate guide to good fishing. Typical notes should include stream name and section fished, the date, type of water, weather, water temperature, water condition, hatch and time of hatch, feeding activity, feeding time, flies used, and fishing success.

To anticipate the time of the hatch, a general rule to follow is: *mayflies will emerge at the most pleasant time of day for the season.* In the spring, this period occurs in the afternoon, usually from 1:00 P.M. to 4:00 P.M., but as the days get warmer, the flies tend to hatch both earlier and later in the day. During hot, muggy weather there will be hatches in the evening and early morning. Then, as summer fades, the morning hatches will appear later and later in the day until fall, when afternoon hatches are again the rule. Once you learn when the individual hatches occur, you can plan your streamside arrival to coincide with the peak fishing period of the day.

Probably the most important attribute of a really successful fly-fisherman is common sense. It should be quite obvious that if we are to simulate the main food source of the trout, we must learn all we can about aquatic insect life. In order to produce effective imitations, it would seem evident that specimens must be caught and examined closely. Also, we must study the activities and habitat of the various species in order to present our artificials in a convincing manner. These are undoubtedly sound and logical procedures, though unfortunately very few fishermen pursue such a course of action. Very little effort is actually required to develop these effective streamside methods, and much is to be gained.

Date_____ No.___

Stream_____ Section_____ Type: Fast___Med___Slow___

Time Fished: 6AM   Noon   6PM   Midnight   6AM
                /_____/_____/_____/_____/ Total Hours_____

Weather: Hot___Cool___Sunny___Cloudy___Rainy___Windy___Stormy___ Temp: Hi___Lo___

Water Conditions: Temp: Hi___Lo___Clear___Discolored___ Level: High___Med___Lo___

Hatches: Species   Activity   Stage   Time

Fishing: Feeding Activity   Time   Artificial   Method

Fish Released: No___ Brooks___Browns___Rainbows___Others___ Size Range_____

Miscellaneous:

Sketches of Effective Imitations:

A blank page from our streamside record book

CHAPTER 7

The Early Season

DURING THE EARLY SEASON, the most pleasant time of day for both the angler and the trout is in the afternoon; this is the time when all the important hatches occur, so we can also call this period the "season of the afternoon hatches." In late April and early May, the water temperature will often drop into the low 40s during the night, causing the trout's metabolism to be very inactive. Then, as the morning sun hits the water, the temperature will rise slowly and hit a peak in the early afternoon. When the 50° mark is reached, the trout's metabolism is raised to a point where good feeding activity can take place. Occasionally fish will feed at a temperature slightly under this figure, but increased activity results when the thermometer climbs to a higher level.

Of course, if the weather is unseasonably warm, minimum feeding conditions may occur as early as 11:00 A.M. moving up the hatch accordingly; but in general, at the start of the early season, the major hatching activity takes place during the afternoon, with the peak period coming between 2:00 and 4:00 P.M. Major spinner falls usually occur soon after this period. As the weather becomes warmer, the hatches and spinner falls get later and later until such flies as *Ephemerella dorothea,* which began as an early-afternoon hatch, become an evening hatch, and the Hendrickson spinner falls are at dusk. The beginning of the hotter weather, usually around the first week in June, marks the start of the midseason.

In Michigan there are likely to be three mayflies on the water Opening Day, which is during the last week in April. These species include *Baetis vagans, Paraleptophlebia adoptiva,* and *Ephemerella subvaria.* In the East, where the season begins slightly earlier, Opening Day anglers will probably run into hatches of both *Epeorus pleuralis* and *Paraleptophlebia adoptiva.* These are all midday to early-afternoon hatches, coming when the water temperature reaches its daily peak. During this part of the season, hatch-oriented anglers need not be concerned about hitting the stream before late morning or noon. As the season progresses, such major species as *Ephemerella dorothea, Leptophlebia cupida,* and *Stenonema vicarium* can emerge both earlier and later as water temperatures rise but, in general, the flies of the early season provide pleasant daytime fishing.

As the water reaches optimum temperature, flies begin to appear and on rich, varied rivers there are often multiple hatches in the afternoon. Sometimes two to three species of mayfly hatch at once and the fish can be very selective, not always choosing the larger, or what appears to be the most numerous species. When you include all of the other insects—caddis flies, stone flies and midges—it can be difficult to determine what the fish prefer. On a single river, fish in one type of habitat may be exposed to more of a certain species than fish in another type of water, and they will feed accordingly. For instance, a slow stretch may have mostly *Paraleptophlebia adoptivia,* and fish in these areas will be keyed to them. In faster areas, *Ephemerella subvaria* will be more numerous, and trout under these lines of drift will want a good Hendrickson imitation. It is important to study the emergence charts in order to be prepared for overlapping hatches and selective trout.

We have talked about smooth-flowing rich rivers, but some, such as the Rogue in Michigan, are almost embarrassingly rich. On a warm May afternoon, it can have stone flies, two species of caddis fly, midges, two or three species of mayfly, and a couple of crane flies, all at once. This situation produces a tremendous amount of feeding activity, but also can pose quite a complicated problem. With the possibility that the trout are feeding on either nymphs, pupas, emerging duns, floating duns or spinners, the angler has the perplexing problem of choosing from among up to fifty patterns. One must be alert and observant, otherwise by the time all fifty patterns have been tried, willy-nilly, hit or miss, the hatch will be over.

In order to identify and then simulate each species properly, we have listed all available data concerning the early season flies. The same procedure will be followed in the two succeeding chapters pertaining to the midseason and the late season. This data will include the insect's scientific name, common name, emergence date, size, nymphal habitat, description of the natural in its various stages, description of the corresponding artificials, and any available information regarding technique and procedures.

Since emergence dates vary slightly depending upon locality, the best procedure, ultimately, is to compile your own hatching chart for the rivers you fish most.

Blue-wing Olive (E, M, W)

Genus and Species	*Baetis* (all species)
Family	*Baetidae*
Emergence	April 1 to October 30
Size	4 to 10 mm (#14 to #24 hook size)
Nymph Habitat	shallow gravel runs and submerged vegetation

NATURAL	*ARTIFICIAL*

NYMPH

NATURAL	ARTIFICIAL
Body brown or olive brown	**Body** dark brown or medium olive and medium brown rabbit fur mixed
Wing Pads blackish	**Wing Pads** black ostrich clump or black crow quill segment
Tails 3, olive brown	**Tails** wood duck or merganser dyed olive
Legs olive brown	**Legs** wood duck or merganser dyed olive

DUN

NATURAL	ARTIFICIAL
Body olive or olive brown	**Body** medium olive or medium olive and medium brown rabbit fur mixed
Wings light or medium gray	**Wings** light or medium gray hen hackle fibers, clump
Tails 2 (except tricaudatus), light gray or whitish, typical	**Tails** light gray hackle fibers
Legs light gray or whitish, typical	**Hackle** none or light gray, parachute

SPINNER

NATURAL	ARTIFICIAL
Body medium or dark brown	**Body** medium or dark brown rabbit fur
Wings hyaline	**Wings** light gray hen hackle tips, spent
Tails 2, (except tricaudatus) light gray or whitish, typical	**Tails** light gray hackle fibers
Legs light gray or whitish, typical	**Hackle** none

The *Baetis* group or Blue-wing Olives provide some of the most prolific hatching activity on rivers and streams across the country. They are not only widespread, but are on the water all season long. We have witnessed beautiful hatches of *Baetis tricaudatus* in Colorado during the month of March and of *Baetis hiemalis* on Michigan streams in mid-November. In both cases the trout were feeding heavily on the emerging duns.

The features and coloration of *Baetis* are so similar that in many cases identification at the species level can only be determined by an entomologist. For the fly-fishermen, then, it will be much more practical to cover the numerous Blue-wing Olives as one group. In general this group can be divided into two fairly distinct color types. This holds true not only for the duns but also for the nymphs and spinners.

Most duns fall into either the light-gray wing–olive body or medium gray–olive-brown body classification. Nymphs are generally brown or olive brown, while spinners are medium or dark brown. For the angler who wants to keep his *Baetis* patterns to a minimum, the best approach would be to carry duns with olive-brown bodies and medium-gray wings, nymphs with olive-brown bodies, and spinners with bodies spun from a combination

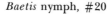

Baetis nymph, #20

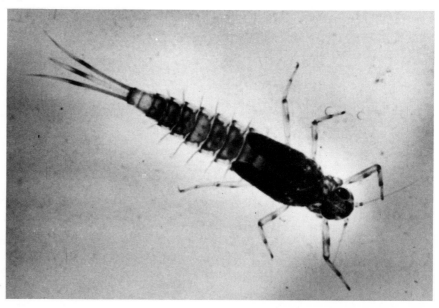

of medium- and dark-brown fur. This procedure follows the theory that the trout picks out the color he wants to see. This theory may or may not be valid, but we've found it to be generally effective for numerous hatches. If this approach is followed, use two parts of medium-olive fur to one part of medium brown for the dun body. This keeps the pattern light enough for species such as *pygmaeus* and *levitans*, yet provides enough brown to work for the darker species such as *vagans* and *cingulatus*. Also use medium-gray wing material. A wing that is too dark normally works much better than one that is too light.

All *Baetis* nymphs are either olive, brown, or olive brown. For a single pattern then, it is best to mix one part medium-olive fur to one part medium-brown fur. The same applies to the spinner. Mix medium- and dark-brown fur, one to one.

The nymphs of *Baetis* are streamlined and very vigorous swimmers, so patterns should be slender and fished with lots of action. Nymphal and emerging imitations are quite effective just before and during the hatch. For the smaller species, sizes #20 to #24, excellent wing cases for the nymph, can be fashioned by spinning on a clump of blackish, fine-textured fur, such as mole. More realism is added by picking the fur slightly. For the emerging pattern, use tiny dark-gray hackle tips to replace the wing pad material.

Baetis duns can be found on the water anytime of the season and most anytime of day, especially from 11:00 A.M. until dusk. A few species are comparatively large in size, #14 and #16, but most are in the 4- to 6-mm category, or #20 to #24. Too often, because of their size, they are completely ignored by the angler. In early May, for example, *Baetis vagans* is found on the water simultaneously with the slightly larger *Paraleptophlebia adoptiva* and the much larger Hendricksons. If they appear in significantly greater numbers, the fish will feed on them heartily. Many times the fisherman will think the larger species is what the trout are taking when they are actually feeding on the small *Baetis*. A parallel situation exists when the *cingulatus* hatch is on during late May and early June. The duns of this species emerge along with the larger and better known *Ephemerella dorothea*, though on many occasions the trout seem to prefer the smaller fly. These duns are very minute, size #20 and #22, and can be extremely difficult to see, especially when they are mixed in with the size #16 Sulphurs.

The hen-hackle fibers used for the wings of the subimago pattern are easier to tie and also form a more definite outline if they are clipped to shape after mounting. Equally effective wing materials include turkey breast, duck shoulders, and quill segments.

Spinners of the East and Midwestern species normally return to the water during the late afternoon and evening while Western species prefer either early morning or evening flights. Some females have the peculiar habit of crawling or diving underwater to lay their eggs, making both wet and dry patterns important. The wet imago is tied on a slightly heavier hook with the wings slanted more to the rear.

Quill Gordon (E)

Genus and Species	*Epeorus pleuralis*
Family	*Heptageniidae*
Other Common Names	Gordon Quill
	Dark Gordon Quill
Emergence	April 20 to May 20
Size	9 to 11 mm (#12 to #14 hook size)
Nymph Habitat	swift gravel or rocky riffles

NATURAL	ARTIFICIAL

NYMPH

NATURAL	ARTIFICIAL
Body dark grayish brown	**Body** gray and brown rabbit fur mixed
Wing Pads brownish black	**Wing Pads** black ostrich clump
Tails 2, tannish with dark flecks	**Tails** wood duck
Legs tannish with brown mottling	**Legs** wood duck

DUN

NATURAL	ARTIFICIAL
Body yellowish with dark brown markings	**Body** pale yellow and dark brown rabbit fur mixed
Wings dark gray	**Wings** dark gray duck-quill segments
Tails 2, tannish	**Tails** ginger, widely spread
Legs tannish with dark brown markings	**Hackle** sparse bronze blue-dun or none

SPINNER

NATURAL	ARTIFICIAL
Body yellowish with dark brown markings	**Body** pale yellow and dark brown rabbit fur mixed
Wings hyaline	**Wings** light blue-dun hen hackle tips, spent
Tails 2, dark brown	**Tails** dark brown hackle fibers
Legs tannish with dark brown markings	**Hackle** none

Emergence of the Quill Gordons usually marks the beginning of good dry-fly fishing for Eastern anglers. This hatch provides excellent early season activity even though the weather may be cold, snowy, and blustery. Our last encounter with *Epeorus pleuralis* occurred at Henryville, with four inches of snow on the ground and a maximum water temperature of slightly less than fifty degrees. Numb fingers combined with pounding hearts produced some of the finest fishing of the season. A blanket of floating duns, unable to warm their muscles enough to escape the lines of drift, caused frenzied feeding for almost two hours. After a long winter of anticipating the first good hatch, this was like a dream come true.

Such episodes are typical of the Quill Gordon hatch. The weather is often cold and uncomfortable, causing many anglers to pass up excellent streamside action in favor of fireside activities. Most fishermen find it diffi-

Epeorus nymph, #16

cult to believe that good fly hatches can exist during such miserable weather. By taking advantage of these situations one soon learns to look forward to the so-called miserable weather rather than dreading it.

The nymphs of *Epeorus pleuralis* are generally found where fast-water situations prevail. They have large distinct gills that are utilized as suction cups for clinging to rocks and stones, even in the swiftest of currents. When emergence time approaches, the nymphs migrate to the downstream side of underwater objects where the nymphal skin is cast off. The newly hatched dun ascends, pierces the surface film, and then floats along to dry bedraggled wings.

This peculiar type of underwater hatching makes an emerging pattern very effective, at least during the initial stages of the hatch. The emerging artificial is tied similarly to the no-hackle dun except that a heavy wire hook is used and the duck-quill wings are shorter and slanted more to the rear. It is best fished by casting upstream, allowing it to sink, and then twitching it up through the currents in front of feeding fish. The emerging pattern should also be tied on light wire hooks for use when the trout become more conscious of surface feeding. Sometimes it works well through the rest of the hatch. A time usually comes, however, when only a high-riding, upright-wing dun will work. The duck-quill segment pattern listed is excellent, but other wing materials, such as duck shoulder and turkey breast are equally effective. The turkey-wing version is best tied in a clump with a few turns of parachute hackle.

The imagos return during the middle of the day and on occasion can be quite important, especially on warmer days. An alternate spinner pattern can be tied using bronze blue-dun hackle or light blue-dun hackle, clipped top and bottom.

Slate-winged Mahogany Dun (E, M)

Genus and Species	*Paraleptophlebia adoptiva*
Family	Leptophlebiidae
Emergence	April 20 to June 15
Size	7 to 9 mm (#16 to #18 hook size)
Nymph Habitat	shallow gravel-bottomed areas

NATURAL	ARTIFICIAL
NYMPH	
Body medium to dark brown	**Body** dark and medium brown rabbit fur mixed
Wing Pads black	**Wing Pads** black crow quill segment
Tails 3, tannish olive	**Tails** wood duck
Legs tannish olive	**Legs** wood duck
DUN	
Body reddish brown with olive cast	**Body** reddish brown and light olive rabbit fur mixed
Wings slate gray	**Wings** dark gray duck shoulder
Tails 3, brown	**Tails** brown hackle fibers
Legs brown	**Hackle** dark bronze blue-dun v hackle or none
SPINNER	
Body dark reddish brown	**Body** dark reddish-brown fur
Wings hyaline	**Wings** bronze blue-dun hackle, clipped top and bottom
Tails 3, grayish brown	**Tails** bronze blue-dun hackle fibers
Legs brownish	**Hackle** none

These little mahogany-bodied duns make up one of the earliest hatches of the season both in the East and Midwest. They often appear on the water with other larger species, such as *Ephemerella subvaria,* and close observance is required to discover which is being taken. Many times the angler will assume that the fish are feeding on the larger fly, when they are actually preferring the *adoptiva* duns.

Emergence takes place at the surface, making the use of an emerging pattern very effective when fished dead-drift over rising trout. This fly is fashioned by substituting dark gray hackle points for the wing pads of the nymphal dressing. A light wire hook should be used to provide proper flotation.

The hatching activity usually begins around 11:00 A.M., and continues sporadically all afternoon. In very cold weather the duns will ride the water a long distance due to cold wing muscles that must be warmed sufficiently before flight can occur. The spinners return around midday and can be important when they are most numerous on water.

Cast skin of
Paraleptophlebia adoptiva

Hendrickson (E, M)

Genus and Species	*Ephemerella subvaria*
Family	Ephemerellidae
Other Common Names	Beaverkill
	Borchers
Emergence	April 25 to June 15
Size	9 to 12 mm (#12 to #14 hook size)
Nymph Habitat	swift gravel riffles of any size stream

NATURAL / ARTIFICIAL

NYMPH

NATURAL	ARTIFICIAL
Body dark chestnut brown	**Body** dark reddish brown rabbit fur
Wing Pads brownish black	**Wing Pads** black ostrich clump
Tails 3, amber with dark bands	**Tails** wood duck
Legs amber with dark bands	**Legs** wood duck

DUN

NATURAL	ARTIFICIAL
Body various combinations of olive, tan, and yellow	**Body** tan, olive, and yellow rabbit fur mixed
Wings medium to dark gray	**Wings** dark gray mallard shoulder
Tails 3, light olive with dark flecks	**Tails** bronze blue-dun hackle fibers, widely spread
Legs light olive with dark flecks	**Hackle** sparse dark blue-dun v hackle or none

SPINNER

NATURAL	ARTIFICIAL
Body dark chestnut brown	**Body** chestnut brown rabbit or buffalo fur
Wings hyaline	**Wings** light gray hen-hackle tips, spent
Tails 3, light olive with dark flecks	**Tails** bronze blue-dun hackle fibers
Legs olive brown	**Hackle** none

Peak emergence in Michigan is from May 5 to May 15, and slightly earlier in the East, and later in the colder streams. *Ephemerella subvaria* closely resemble *Ephemerella invaria* and *Ephemerella rotunda,* but E. *subvaria* has better defined abdominal spines as a nymph, darker wings as a dun, and darker body and wing veins as a spinner. Also, E. *subvaria* has passed its peak before others come on in good numbers.

The nymphs become active around noon and imitations should be fished deep and dead-drift with an occasional twitching motion. Emergence begins around 2:00 P.M., so it's wise to put on an emerging pattern just prior to this period. It should be fished shallow or in the film, and also requires a gentle twitching action. Even when the duns start popping up, the emerging pattern can be used effectively well into the hatch, though as the fish become more selective it will cease to produce, and the dun imitation is required. The most essential requirement of the dun is a wing that closely simulates the size, color, and silhouette of the natural. It is imperative that the artificial land on the water with its wings in an upright position. This is one of the most significant features of the floating dun.

Depending on weather conditions, the hatch may last thirty minutes to three hours, but about two hours is normal. Often, during an early May afternoon, we get Chimarra caddis flies, *Baetis vagans,* and *Paraleptophlebia adoptiva,* along with *Ephemerella subvaria.* You must be alert to discover which species the fish are rising to. Individual fish in different areas sometimes display different tastes. This is due to the numerical abundance of one species over others in a particular location. The smaller flies are less discernible to the fisherman, although there may be more of them.

On warm afternoons in early May the spinners fall in the water about 4:00 to 5:00 P.M., lying flush in the film, and become almost invisible. If the fish resume feeding after the hatch is over, they are probably feeding on the spinners. The rise form is now much less hurried and more regular and deliberate than the splashing noisy feeding to the duns. As the days get warmer, the spinner fall gets later and later, until eventually it comes at dusk. The spinner fall is more concentrated than the emergence and lasts only about thirty minutes, but a good imitation produces some of the best fish. A good Hendrickson spinner fall is something to remember. Every trout in the stream seems to take part in the feeding activity. As compared to the difficulty encountered with some other species, this is relatively easy fishing. Imitations of the imago are simple to fashion, but it's important to carry patterns displaying two or three wing silhouettes. Some of the naturals floating down will have upright wings, some spent wings, and some half-spent wings. Full hackle will imitate the upright version while the others require trimming. If you prefer tying only one pattern, tie the full hackle variety and carry scissors in your vest. We like the hen-wing spinner best when the naturals are full spent. Light hooks and top-quality hackles are an absolute necessity for the proper flotation of the full-spent and half-spent artificials.

Coloration of the Hendrickson dun can vary tremendously from stream to stream—in fact, even from different areas on the same stream. The suggested pattern for the subimago has a body constructed of yellow, tan, and olive fur, which is normally effective, but should actually be matched to the naturals being imitated. For the wings, the proper shade of gray should be selected from the mallard shoulder area. The feathers chosen can be used either natural or trimmed to shape. Turkey-breast feathers, dyed and cut, also make durable and highly effective wings. If hackle is not utilized on the pattern, then the tail fibers must be spread widely to act as outriggers. This feature ensures that the fly will land on the water in an upright position.

Black Quill (E, M)

Genus and Species	*Leptophlebia cupida*
Family	Leptophlebiidae
Other Common Names	Whirling Dun
	Early Brown Spinner
Emergence	April 25 to August 15
Size	10 to 12 mm (#12 to #14 hook size)
Nymph Habitat	slow current and backwaters, in leaf drift or silt and trash-covered areas

NATURAL | *ARTIFICIAL*

NYMPH

NATURAL	ARTIFICIAL
Body dark brown	**Body** dark brown rabbit fur
Wing Pads blackish	**Wing Pads** black crow quill segment
Tails 3, brown	**Tails** dark brown mallard breast
Legs brown	**Legs** dark brown mallard breast

DUN

NATURAL	ARTIFICIAL
Body dark brown	**Body** dark brown rabbit fur
Wings slate gray washed with brown	**Wings** dark elk hair, clump
Tails 3, light olive brown	**Tails** dark bronze blue dun
Legs olive brown	**Hackle** dark bronze blue dun, parachute

SPINNER

NATURAL	ARTIFICIAL
Body dark reddish brown	**Body** dark reddish brown seal or buffalo fur
Wings hyaline	**Wings** Bronze blue-dun hen tips, spent
Tails 3, grayish brown	**Tails** dark bronze blue dun
Legs medium brown	**Hackle** none

Peak emergence of this species occurs during mid-May, but sparse, sporadic hatches may be found throughout the greater portion of the season. The nymphs are easy to recognize by their large double, platelike gills. They do not burrow, but instead clamber about on the stream bottom using their camouflage for protection. At hatch time they either crawl out on a log or stone or, in quiet backwaters, shed their skin at the surface. In general, the nymphal pattern has not been too deadly for us, but on occasion a slightly, weighted version used with a sinking line has been effective.

The duns emerge rather sporadically starting at midday and continuing through the afternoon hours. The spinners form their flights during mid to late afternoon and may be found on the water until dusk. These flies are seldom present in great numbers, but due to their size, offer an enticing meal for the trout.

Leptophlebia cupida, from underwater

Gray Fox, American March Brown, Light Cahill (E, M)

Genus and Species	*Stenonema fuscum, S. vicarium, S. ithaca*
Family	Heptageniidae
Other Common Names	Ginger Quill
Emergence	May 10 to July 15
Size	10 to 16 mm (#10, #12 and #14 hook size)
Nymph Habitat	moderate to rapid current, clinging to the underside of stones, in leaf drift or gravel riffles

NATURAL | *ARTIFICIAL*

NYMPH

NATURAL	ARTIFICIAL
Body medium brown to dark brown on top, amber underneath	**Body** dark brown and light brown rabbit fur mixed
Wing Pads dark brown	**Wing Pads** dark brown mottled turkey quill segment
Tails 3, brownish	**Tails** brown mallard breast fibers
Legs amber banded with brown	**Legs** brown mallard breast fibers

DUN

NATURAL	ARTIFICIAL
Body various; tannish mottled with brown, typical	**Body** cream German fitch and brown rabbit fur mixed
Wings tannish olive mottled with dark brown	**Wings** mallard breast feathers dyed tannish olive, clump
Tails 2, amber mottled with brown	**Tails** brown hackle fibers
Legs amber banded brown	**Hackle** honey, parachute

SPINNER

NATURAL	ARTIFICIAL
Body various; tannish mottled with brown, typical	**Body** cream German fitch and brown rabbit fur mixed
Wings hyaline, light brown mottlings	**Wings** bronze blue-dun hackle and sparse grizzly, clipped top and bottom
Tails 2, mottled brown	**Tails** brown hackle fibers
Legs amber banded with brown	**Hackle** none

These large mayflies are important in the East and of local importance in the Midwest. When present in good numbers they normally bring out some of the better fish and cause heavy feeding activity. Duns can hatch in the afternoon, especially on dark cloudy days, although emergence is more often at dusk. Nymphs and emerging patterns are highly effective, as it sometimes takes half a minute or more for the dun to escape the nymphal shuck. Struggling slightly under or in the surface film, they provide a very tempting treat for the trout. For the emerging fly, utilize a clump of wood-duck or brown-mallard breast to imitate the sprouting wings. They should be tied short, about two-thirds body length, and laid back at a 45° angle.

Fish this pattern near or in the surface film with a twitching motion, which will simulate the struggle of the natural.

After complete emergence has been accomplished, the duns will float for a long period of time before taking to the air. A commotion is created as they flutter their wings in an effort to leave the water. This disturbance, coupled with their lengthy ride on the water, make these elegant creatures a favorite of large trout.

Stenonema nymph, #14

Sulphur Dun (E, M)

Genus and Species	*Ephemerella dorothea*
Family	Ephemerellidae
Other Common Names	Pale Evening Dun
	Sulphury Dun
	Pale Watery Dun
Size	6 to 9 mm (#16 and #18 hook size)
Emergence	May 15 to July 5
Nymph Habitat	swift gravel runs and riffles

NATURAL	*ARTIFICIAL*

NYMPH

NATURAL	ARTIFICIAL
Body brown with orangish or yellowish cast, heavily freckled or mottled	**Body** brown mixed with yellow or orange rabbit fur
Wing Pads dark brown, freckled with light brown and yellow	**Wing Pads** dark brown turkey quill segment
Tails 3, amber with brown bands	**Tails** wood duck
Legs amber with brown bands	**Legs** wood duck

DUN

NATURAL	ARTIFICIAL
Body yellow, orangish yellow or olive yellow	**Body** yellow, or yellow mixed with either orange or olive rabbit fur
Wings yellowish gray	**Wings** light gray hen hackle fibers, clump
Tails 3, yellowish	**Tails** honey hackle fibers
Legs yellowish	**Hackle** honey, parachute

SPINNER

NATURAL	ARTIFICIAL
Body yellowish brown	**Body** brown and yellow rabbit fur mixed
Wings hyaline	**Wings** light gray hackle
Tails 3, yellowish	**Tails** honey hackle fibers
Legs yellowish	**Hackle** none

This hatch provides some of the most pleasant fishing of the entire season. The duns can begin their emergence as early as midday, when the water is still cold, and continue for three to five hours. As the season progresses and temperatures rise, the hatch will commence in the mid to late afternoon and continue until almost dusk. By late June, emergence occurs just before sundown and will sometimes last for an hour or so afterward. When the sulphurs are in their daytime phase the emergence is normally sporadic and drawn out, lasting for several hours or more. This situation creates a condition in which the fish are extremely selective and pattern is of utmost importance. Some of the duns have yellow bodies while others are yellow mixed with varying degrees of orange or olive, and as a result, artificials dressed with these three body colorations should be carried during this hatch. The light-gray hen-hackle-fiber wings have been specified in the suggested pattern, but it is also advisable to try duck-shoulder feathers.

The nymphs become very active at hatch time and the fish feed heavily, picking the naturals off the bottom before they can swim to the surface. Heavy wire patterns or sinking lines are a must during these periods. Artificials should be twitched right on the bottom for best results. An emerging pattern can be fashioned by replacing the wing cases on the nymph with medium-gray hackle tips. This fly is sometimes very effective during the entire hatch period. One important suggestion when fishing the nymphal or emerging pattern is to work downstream and use a downstream dead-drift float. This technique is especially effective on the sulphur hatch and is probably due to the orientation of the natural in the surface film. Very few hatches provide as many problems of imitation as this one, and the best way to cope with this situation is to carry a wide variety of imitations and to be creative.

The spinners return at or slightly after dusk and are well imitated with a fur body and wound hackle wings. Full-hackle and trimmed-hackle wing patterns should both be available for the spinner fall. The full hackle provides superior flotation, but the spent and half-spent versions are often necessary for proper simulation. Two other patterns are extremely effective during the dusk and after-dark spinner falls. One utilizes light-gray hen-hackle points, tied one-half or fully spent, with no hackle. The other has wings made from a clump of light-gray partridge, which is split and figure-eighted into the spent or semispent position. A couple turns of undersize bronze blue-dun hackle completes the dressing.

Light Cahill (E, M)

Genus and Species	*Stenomena canadense*
	Stenomena frontale
	Stenomena interpunctatum
	Stenomena heterotarsale
	Stenomena tripunctatum
	Stenomena rubrum
Family	Heptageniidae
Other Common Names	Cream Mays
	Yellow Mays
Emergence	May 15 to August 15
Size	8 to 11 mm (#12 and #14 hook size)
Nymph Habitat	moderate to rapid current in shallow riffles, under stones and detritus

NATURAL	ARTIFICIAL

NYMPH

NATURAL	ARTIFICIAL
Body dark brown on top, pale brownish olive underneath	**Body** med. brown and light olive rabbit fur mixed
Wing Pads dark brown	**Wing Pads** mottled dark brown turkey quill segment
Tails 3, medium brown	**Tails** mallard flank feather, dyed brown
Legs banded light and dark brown	**Legs** mallard flank feather, dyed brown

DUN

NATURAL	ARTIFICIAL
Body various; from creamy white to tannish to pale yellowish olive	**Body** blended fur to match naturals in your area, cream or pale yellowish olive, dyed rabbit fur typical
Wings mottled; creamy, tannish, whitish or yellowish	**Wings** natural mallard flank feathers typical
Tails 2, tan or cream	**Tails** honey hackle fibers
Legs pale amber to white banded with brown	**Hackle** honey, parachute

SPINNER

NATURAL	ARTIFICIAL
Body tannish with an amber cast is typical, but can vary from whitish to orangish yellow	**Body** blended fur to match naturals in your area, cream or pale yellowish rabbit fur typical
Wings hyaline, slight dark mottlings	**Wings** bronze blue-dun hackle and sparse grizzly, clipped top and bottom
Tails 2, tan or cream	**Tails** ginger hackle fibers
Legs tannish banded with brown	**Hackle** none

The duns of this closely related group hatch over a large portion of the season, reaching their peak in the East from mid-June to mid-July and in the Midwest during late July and early August. They are similar in appearance, both as to size and coloration. Most of the subimagos are some shade of yellowish olive, while the others vary from creamy white to a tannish color.

Heaviest hatching periods occur just before dark, but sporadic activity can take place during midday and afternoon. If the fish feed on them at all, it is usually right at dusk. Unfortunately, these flies are rarely on the water in great enough numbers to cause heavy surface feeding. They normally emerge when other, more important species are hatching in greater numbers. Occasionally, however, when they are the predominant insect on the water, excellent dry-fly fishing is experienced. The fish do not seem to be very selective at these times, due probably to the sparseness of the hatch. The spinners return at dusk and ride the water for a considerable distance before depositing their eggs. This means that the angler must decide which stage the fish are feeding on and carry both dun and spinner patterns.

CHAPTER 8

The Midseason

HATCHES OF THE MIDSEASON represent a transition from afternoon activity to evening and night emergence. As the days become warm, early morning activity also begins to develop. In fact, we could call this the season of the "dusk and dawn hatches." The same general rule concerning the hatch periods, that applied to the early season, applies to the midseason. Decide what time of day is the most pleasant for you, and that is usually the best time for the emergence to take place. In the heat of summer, the most pleasant time for man is the cool of early morning or late evening.

This is the season of giant mayflies, such as the Green Drake (*Ephemera guttulata*), the Brown Drake (*Ephemera simulans*), and the enormous Michigan mayfly (*Hexagenia limbata*). These large Ephemerids bring out the "old lunkers" that rarely feed on the surface. Fish over five pounds are not uncommon. They are called "washers" in the Jordan River area of Michigan, because when they rise to a *Hexagenia limbata,* it sounds like a hog falling in the water, with the waves washing up on both banks. Explosive hatches of huge duns and tremendous spinner falls, with females writhing on the surface to expel egg sacs, make old cannibal trout lose all caution and feed almost between the angler's feet.

Not to be ignored are the smaller species in the #18 to #24 size range, which come in the early morning from sunup to about 10:00 A.M. The "washers" will not be on the prowl at this time, but great numbers of ten-to eighteen-inch fish will be rising freely to the smaller flies. This light-tackle fishing is just as much, or more fun, than the night fishing and, during this season, you can enjoy both.

Green Drake, Coffin Fly (E)

Genus and Species	*Ephemera guttulata*
Family	Ephemeridae
Emergence	May 20 to June 15
Size	18 to 22 mm (#8 and #10 hook size)
Nymph Habitat	nymphs burrow in mud banks and silted areas

NATURAL	ARTIFICIAL

NYMPH

NATURAL	ARTIFICIAL
Body amber with distinct olive cast	**Body** creamy-tan German fitch and light olive rabbit fur mixed
Wing Pads dark brown	**Wing Pads** dark brown ostrich clump
Tails 3, light olive	**Tails** light partridge dyed olive, short
Legs tannish olive	**Legs** light partridge dyed olive

DUN

NATURAL	ARTIFICIAL
Body creamy yellow with brownish markings	**Body** light deer or elk body hair, tinted yellow, extended, brown thread ribbing
Wings light gray with distinct olive cast and brown mottlings	**Wings** clump of deer or elk body hair tinted olive
Tails 3, dark brownish-olive	**Tails** moose mane or pheasant tail fibers
Legs creamish with brownish markings	**Hackle** dark ginger and grizzly, parachute

SPINNER

NATURAL	ARTIFICIAL
Body light cream, brown markings on thorax	**Body** light cream deer body hair, extended, white thread ribbing
Wings hyaline, heavily mottled with dark brown markings	**Wings** clump of dark brown elk hair, sparse
Tails 3, brown	**Tails** moose mane or pheasant tail fibers
Legs yellowish, forelegs brown	**Hackle** bronze blue dun, parachute

For many Eastern anglers, the *Ephemera guttulata* hatch is the peak of excitement for the entire season. Just the sight of one Green Drake struggling on the surface of a placid pool is enough to quicken the heartbeat and bring about a feeling of great anticipation. This is the period when many of the old lunkers come out of their hiding places and feed freely on the surface. At no other time of the season are such large trout so susceptible to the dry fly.

The nymphs of *guttulata* belong to the family Ephemeridae and are characterized by legs flanged for burrowing, mandibles bearing long tusks, and fringed, feathery gills. They are usually found among the silt and debris that collect around rocks and large boulders and also in the mudbanks of quiet backwaters. At hatch time, they crawl out of their burrows and swim rapidly to the surface, where the dun emerges almost instantly. During this period, a nymphal pattern fished in such a manner is very deadly. Simulation of this phenomenon can best be accomplished by sinking a heavy-wire imitation to the bottom and then utilizing a high-rod technique to swing it quickly to the surface. Further realism can be augmented by using a quick, but subtle, wrist action to impart an undulating movement to the artificial.

The emerging pattern for *guttulata* should be tied on lighter wire hooks and fished in the film. To construct this imitation, use the nymphal dressing, except for the wing pads, which instead should be a clump of four dark-gray hackle points tied short. A twitching action should be used to simulate the struggle of shedding the nymphal shuck.

Heaviest emergence of these olive-tinted duns comes in the evening, but sporadic activity can occur throughout the afternoon. They encounter great difficulty in getting off the water, creating quite a commotion as they struggle along making numerous unsuccessful efforts to fly. This characteristic, combined with their extremely large size, makes *Ephemera guttulata* an almost irresistible morsel for even the most wary old lunker. When on the water in great abundance, as they often are, the Green Drake duns can cause big trout to throw caution to the wind and to feed voraciously. Most anglers make a great effort to produce drag-free, dead-drift floats when using the dry fly, but the Green Drake is one of many hatches where a well-executed twitch is not only permissible but very deadly.

Both of the suggested dun and spinner patterns have extended hair bodies, hair-clump wings and parachute hackle. We've found this type of pattern to be quite effective when imitating the larger mayflies. Another artificial that looks promising, but needs more field testing, is the two-feather mayfly type. This fly is tied on a short-shank hook and consists of only two feathers, a duck-breast feather and a hackle. The breast feather is utilized as the body, wings, and tail and then the hackle is wound parachute around the wings.

The effectiveness of these two types of dressing is probably due to the way the fly floats in the water rather than close duplication of color. Parachute hackle keeps them floating upright and allows the body to make proper contact with the water.

The spinners of *guttulata,* more commonly known as Coffin Flies, normally return at dusk three days after emergence. It is quite a spectacular sight to watch them swarm high over the stream and gradually dip lower and lower toward the water's surface. When the egg-laying process commences, trout of all sizes are excited into frenzied feeding activity. Once a good riser is located, he should be stalked and tested without hesitation. Time and effort must be put to maximum use as these periods are often short lived, and due to the relatively large size of the naturals, much less feeding is required to satisfy even the largest appetites.

Large Mahogany Dun (E, M)

Genus and Species	*Isonychia bicolor*
Family	Baetidae
Other Common Names	Leadwing Coachman
	Dun Variant
	Slate Drake
	White-Gloved Howdy
Emergence	May 20 to September 20
Size	13 to 16 mm (#10 and #12 hook size)
Nymph Habitat	moderate to swift currents

NATURAL	ARTIFICIAL

NYMPH

NATURAL	ARTIFICIAL
Body dark brown	**Body** dark brown rabbit
Wing Pads blackish	**Wing Pads** black ostrich clump
Tails 3, medium brown	**Tails** medium brown mallard breast
Legs light olive, brown bands	**Legs** wood duck

DUN

NATURAL	ARTIFICIAL
Body dark reddish brown	**Body** reddish brown rabbit fur
Wings dark slate	**Wings** dark gray elk hair, clump
Tails 2, tan	**Tails** light brown hackle fibers
Legs forelegs brown, middle and hindlegs cream	**Hackle** bronze blue dun, parachute

SPINNER

NATURAL	ARTIFICIAL
Body reddish brown	**Body** reddish brown rabbit fur
Wings hyaline	**Wings** light gray hen hackle tips
Tails 2, cream	**Tails** ginger hackle fibers
Legs forelegs brownish, feet white on female, middle and hindlegs cream	**Hackle** none

This large mayfly is found both in the East and Midwest, but seems more important to Eastern anglers. We've encountered sporadic hatches on Michigan's Au Sable system; however, we've seen nothing to compare with those on Art Flick's Schoharie. Degradation of the Green Drake hatch in recent years has made the Slate Wing one of the most important large trout hatches of the season.

The emergence period is very long, from late May to late September, but usually peaks during mid-June in the East and mid-July in Michigan. Nymphs of *Isonychia* are long, streamlined, and are vigorous swimmers. When emergence time approaches, they swim into shallow, quieter water, usually along the banks, and crawl out on stones to hatch. The trout are aware of this migration and follow along for an easy meal. Nymphal imitations fished in a like manner can be very productive during this period.

Owing to this method of emergence, the duns are relatively less available to the trout than for most other hatches. A fair number, however, do manage to fall or get blown into the water. This fact, coupled with their large size and tendency to struggle on the surface, makes the Large Mahogany Duns a special treat for the trout. The hatch comes in the evening during sunny, seasonable weather, but may occur during daylight hours on cloudy days.

The imagos return in the evening, causing a situation where both duns and spinners are on the water at the same time. The angler must pay close attention to know which the trout are feeding on.

Duns drifting relatively motionless in the current are best imitated with the elk wing parachute pattern. Deer-body hair dyed dark gray is a good substitute for the elk. When the duns are active, or being blown by the wind, a high-riding hackle fly is deadly. It can be skittered and skated. For this pattern, use dark blue-dun hackle wound conventionally with no wings. High quality dry-fly hackle must be used for both tails and hackle.

Brown Drake (E, M, W)

Genus and Species	*Ephemera simulans*
Family	Ephemeridae
Emergence	May 25 to July 15
Size	10 to 14 mm (#10 and #12 hook size)
Nymph Habitat	stream bottoms with a mixture of sand and gravel

NATURAL	*ARTIFICIAL*
NYMPH	
Body amber with medium brown markings	**Body** creamy tan German fitch and medium brown rabbit fur mixed
Wing Pads dark brownish black	**Wing Pads** dark brown ostrich clump
Tails 3, amber	**Tails** light tan partridge, short
Legs amber	**Legs** light tan partridge
DUN	
Body grayish yellow with dark brown markings	**Body** yellow, light gray and brown rabbit fur mixed
Wings gray, heavily spotted with dark brown	**Wings** dark deer body hair, clump
Tails 3, amber	**Tails** ginger hackle fibers
Legs amber	**Hackle** brown and grizzly, parachute
SPINNER	
Body dark brown, yellowish underneath	**Body** yellow and light brown rabbit fur mixed
Wings hyaline, heavily spotted with dark brownish-black	**Wings** brown and grizzly hackle, full or clipped top and bottom
Tails 3, pale yellowish brown	**Tails** ginger hackle fibers
Legs pale yellowish brown	**Hackle** none

The nymphal pattern is effective just before the hatch and should be fished with a fairly active retrieve. When tied on a light-wire hook and fished in the film, it is also deadly during the initial phase of the emergence. However, the fish soon become partial to the freshly hatched subimagos and, at that point, a dun pattern must be used. The deer-body hair tied in a clump makes an excellent wing outline and provides a perfect base for securing the parachute hackle. An alternate body material for both dun and spinner is deer hair dyed to the proper shade. In Michigan, the Brown Drake is the first large fly of the year that provides good dusk and after-dark fishing. Due to their size and time of emergence, big fish are induced to feed on the surface. The hatch is normally at its peak sometime between June fifth and June fifteenth, a week or so before the even larger *Hexagenia limbata*. Duns and spinners are both on the water from sundown until well after dark, making it difficult to discover which stage the fish are feeding on.

The Brown Drake immediately follows the famous Green Drake, or *Ephemerella grandis*, hatch in the West. Except for a slight size variation, both species look similar on the water. The trout can easily tell the difference, so the angler must be able to recognize the change and act accordingly. Several times we've been fooled by this situation, thinking the fish were taking Green Drakes when they had actually switched to the brown variety. The importance of collecting specimens and examining them in your hand cannot be emphasized enough.

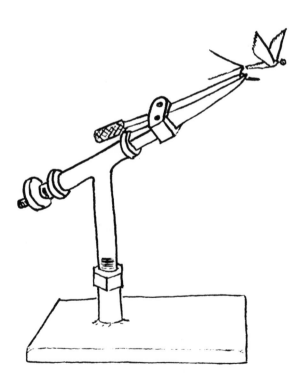

Slate-maroon Drake (W)

Genus and Species	*Epeorus nitidus*
Family	Heptageniidae
Emergence	June 1 to July 15
Size	11 to 14 mm (#12 and #14 hook size)
Nymph Habitat	fast water, rocks, and gravel

NATURAL	*ARTIFICIAL*

NYMPH

NATURAL	*ARTIFICIAL*
Body dark brownish gray with darker mottling on back	**Body** brown and dark gray rabbit fur mixed
Wing Case dark brown	**Wing Cases** very dark brown quill segment
Tails 2, mottled brown	**Tails** brown partridge
Legs mottled brown	**Legs** brown partridge

DUN

NATURAL	*ARTIFICIAL*
Body maroon under, mottled brown on top	**Body** maroon rabbit fur
Wings dark gray	**Wings** dark gray quill segments
Tails 2, gray	**Tails** gray hackle fibers
Legs Gray with brown markings	**Hackle** none

SPINNER

NATURAL	*ARTIFICIAL*
Body yellowish brown, segments 2–7 semi-transparent	**Body** yellow and brown rabbit fur mixed
Wings hyaline with distinct reddish brown veins	**Wings** light gray hen hackle tips, spent
Tails 2, pale yellowish brown	**Tails** honey hackle fibers
Legs amber shading to brown	**Hackle** none

This rather spectacular Ephemerid produces a mid- to late-morning hatch that is normally short in duration but great in number. Fish are attracted to this fat, juicy mayfly which usually creates heavy feeding activity. A weighted nymph fished in the deep runs just before and during the hatch is often deadly. This is a common species found widely over the Western states on both sides of the Continental Divide.

Pale Morning Dun #1 (W)

Genus and Species	*Ephemerella lacustris*
Family	Ephemerellidae
Emergence	June 5 to July 30
Size	7 to 9 mm (#16 and #18 hook size)
Nymph Habitat	gravel, quiet runs, and still water

NATURAL   *ARTIFICIAL*

NYMPH

Body medium brown	**Body** medium brown rabbit fur
Wing Pads dark brown	**Wing Pads** dark brown quill segments
Abdomen brown with dorsal light amber segments on middle of abdomen	
Tails 3, amber mottled with brown	**Tails** dark brown partridge
Legs amber mottled with brown	**Legs** dark brown partridge

DUN

Body male: yellowish orange with a slight olive cast. Female: olive with a slight yellowish cast	**Body** pale yellow and olive rabbit fur mixed
Wings light gray with yellowish tinges on the leading edge	**Wings** light gray duck-shoulder or light gray hen-hackle fibers, clipped to shape
Tails 3, light olive with brown rings	**Tails** light olive hackle fibers
Legs light olive	**Hackle** none or light olive, parachute

SPINNER

Body female: light greenish tan. Male: reddish brown	**Body** light green and light tan rabbit fur, mixed
Wings hyaline	**Wings** light gray hen-hackle tips
Tails 3, light olive with brown rings	**Tails** light olive hackle fibers
Legs light olive	**Hackle** none

Ephemerella lacustris is normally considered a lake species, and is widespread in Yellowstone Lake and some of the lakes of the Centennial Valley in Idaho. However, we have found it common early in the season on many spring creeks. These are usually slow-moving streams with relatively little current. The flies are extremely prevalent on Henrys Fork of the Snake in Idaho, and Armstrong Creek in Montana, and constitute one of the first important hatches of the season in these waters.

Most rivers in the West are high during the spring runoff when this insect emerges. However, the spring creeks do not get high water early in the season, and most of us who prefer dry-fly fishing to rising trout tend to fish these spring creek-type rivers at this time. The naturals emerge before and during the *Ephemerella grandis* hatch.

We have found duns on the water as early as seven in the morning, although the fish do not normally become interested in them until 10:00 to 10:30 A.M., due possibly to typical low morning temperatures. A weighted nymph fished in deep runs during this period is often useful.

Some spinners fall in the morning, but the greater fall seems to be in the evening, from about 6:30 P.M. until dark, often literally carpeting the river. Very large fish will feed on these small spinners. The male spinners have a reddish-brown appearance in the sunlight while the female spinners are more greenish. The duns are imitated by a Paradun or No-Hackle tied with wings from duck-shoulder feathers, and the No-Hackle tied with wings from primary quill segments of a mallard or other duck. These flies often save the day for the dry-fly man who is looking for the Western Green Drake or *Ephemerella grandis,* which often comes at this time. The latter is often spotty and sparse, but the Pale Morning Duns can be relied upon. The nymphs of the *Ephemerella lacustris* closely resemble the nymphs of the Hendrickson (*Ephemerella subvaria*) to which they are closely related. Both have a pale amber section in the center of the upper abdomen. The naturals start their emergence period from early June and continue through most of July. Three closely related Western species, *Ephemerella inermis, Ephemerella infrequens,* and *E. lacustris* all belong to the same subgenus. To the naked eye they could almost be the same insect, except, of course, for the slight difference in size and date of emergence. We have witnessed hatches containing all three species, simultaneously. According to Edmunds, *Ephemerella inermis* may have two or three sibling species. However, from the fisherman's viewpoint, all can be considered Pale Morning Duns. The spinners are also indistinguishable to the naked eye. These species are widespread in the West from Colorado to Montana to California.

Slate-winged Olive (E)

Genus and Species	*Ephemerella attenuata*
Family	Ephemerellidae
Emergence	June 5 to July 5
Size	6 to 9 mm (#16 and #18 hook size)
Nymph Habitat	gravel riffles and slow currents in streams of all sizes

NATURAL	*ARTIFICIAL*

NYMPH

Body tannish brown	**Body** tan and brown rabbit fur mixed
Wing Pads dark brown	**Wing Pads** dark brown orstrich clump
Tails 3, tannish, short	**Tails** tan partridge
Legs tannish mottled with brown	**Legs** brown partridge

DUN

Body medium olive	**Body** medium olive rabbit fur
Wings dark gray, almost black	**Wings** dark gray turkey breast, clump
Tails 3, olive	**Tails** olive hackle fibers
Legs light olive	**Hackle** light olive, parachute

SPINNER

Body thorax dark brown, abdomen medium brown	**Body** dark brown and medium brown rabbit fur mixed
Wings hyaline	**Wings** light gray hen-hackle tips
Tails 3, light olive	**Tails** light olive hackle fibers
Legs light olive	**Hackle** none

Ephemerella attenuata is found only in the East, but is closely related to the Midwestern species, *Ephemerella lata*. To the angler, they can be considered identical, except for one minor difference: coloration of the nymphs. The nymphs of *attenuata* are much lighter, having a distinct tannish cast, as opposed to the much darker *lata*. The duns normally hatch around midday, but can appear sporadically from early morning to late afternoon depending on weather conditions. The marked contrast of blackish wings over bright olive bodies simplifies identification. The spinners return to the water for mating and egg laying at dusk the following day.

Green Drake (W)

Genus and Species	*Ephemerella grandis*
Family	Emphemerellidae
Emergence	June 15 to July 15
Size	14 to 16 mm (#10 and #12 hook size)
Nymph Habitat	medium to fast rock and gravel runs

NATURAL	ARTIFICIAL

NYMPH

NATURAL	ARTIFICIAL
Body dark blackish brown	**Body** dark blackish brown mole fur
Wing Pads black	**Wing Pads** black quill segment
Tails 3, dark brown	**Tails** dark brown partridge
Legs dark brownish black	**Legs** dark brown partridge

DUN

NATURAL	ARTIFICIAL
Body green with dark brown rings—dark brown markings only on dorsal in freshly hatched duns	**Body** medium green deer hair extended body ribbed with dark brown thread
Wings dark slate gray	**Wings** dark elk hair, clump
Tails 3, green and brown	**Tails** olive hackle fibers
Legs light yellowish olive shading to brownish green	**Hackle** olive, parachute, sparse and short

SPINNER

NATURAL	ARTIFICIAL
Body dark brown with wide pale margins so as to appear ringed	**Body** reddish-brown rabbit fur ribbed with light gray muskrat fur
Wings hyaline	**Wings** pale gray hen-hackle tips
Tails 3, dark brown	**Tails** bronze blue-dun hackle fibers
Legs pale tan	**Hackle** none

Ephemerella grandis is one of the largest mayflies found in the West, and on many rivers is the most important hatch of the season. Due to its large size, giant trout can be found feeding on the surface during this hatch. We have landed rainbows up to five pounds at Western Green Drake time and have heard of ten pounders being taken. Many fish eighteen to twenty inches are common during a good day. The nymphs are large, fat, and relished. The hatch seems to start with a few flies coming off in the morning for four or five days. Suddenly the hatch will start in the morning and last until about five in the afternoon, with duns literally covering the water, perhaps one dun for every square foot of water. After two to three days of peak hatching, it will taper off and there will be just a few flies in the

Ephemerella grandis nymph, #10

morning for about a week. On cold cloudy days we have seen this hatch hold off until four in the afternoon and emerge heavily until dark. We have never seen a spinner fall, and knowledgeable guides who fish many rivers in the West, with good Green Drake hatches, have told us that they have never seen a spinner fall either. It probably comes after dark.

Any of our dun patterns work well: the Paradun, the No-Hackle, and especially the extended-body types. An exceptional one is the V Hackle Partridge Drake. The wings are partridge feathers dyed dark gray and tied much the same way as a fan wing, with the hackle tied on normally and clipped on the top and bottom so that the only fibers are coming out the sides.

Local anglers use a conglomeration of large flies such as Goofus Bugs, Grizzly Wolfs, Gray Wolfs and Irresistibles, all of which seem to work fairly well. However, you do get refusals with these flies. Even after the hatch has tapered off, the fish seem to be on the lookout for these large mayflies in the mornings between 10:00 A.M and 1:00 P.M., and large fish can be found rising, cruising, and feeding on the occasional dun. The date for this hatch around the area of West Yellowstone is June 22 to July 4, varying according to altitude and unseasonal weather.

One note on the color of the duns: the freshly hatched female has a bright green body with slight brown markings on the back. However, the same dun one hour later is much darker, mostly dark reddish brown with light olive rings. The fish see the bright green, not the later darker fly. Most species of dun become darker on aging, but in this species the problem was so pronounced it necessitated transporting the camera equipment to the river-bank.

Slate-Brown Dun (W)

Genus and Species	*Epeorus longimanus*
Family	Heptageniidae
Emergence	June 15 to July 15
Size	10 to 11 mm (# 14 hook size)
Nymph Habitat	small to medium size streams above 5,000 feet on large rocks

NATURAL	*ARTIFICIAL*

NYMPH

NATURAL	*ARTIFICIAL*
Body dark grayish brown, light brown underneath	**Body** brownish gray muskrat fur
Wing Pads dark brownish black	**Wing Pads** dark brown or black quill segments
Tails 2, tan with dark brown markings	**Tails** brown partridge fibers
Legs tan with dark markings	**Legs** brown partridge fibers

DUN

NATURAL	*ARTIFICIAL*
Body Light gray with dark markings on the back	**Body** light gray muskrat fur
Wing Pads dark gray	**Wing Pads** dark gray duck-shoulder feathers
Tails 2, gray with brown markings	**Tails** medium gray hackle fibers
Legs tan shading to brown	**Hackle** none

SPINNER

NATURAL	*ARTIFICIAL*
Body pale brownish, although can vary to reddish brown according to locality	**Body** tan beaver or rabbit fur
Wings hyaline	**Wings** light gray hen-hackle tips, spent
Tails 2, tan modeled	**Tails** tan hackle fibers
Legs tan	**Hackle** none

Epeorus species are common in the East and West and rare in the Midwest. The size range of the various species is from 7 to 11 mm. Nymphs are two tailed and flat bodied with a large head. *E. longimanus* is found in small and medium-size streams above 5,000 feet in fast water. They are replaced by *E. albertae* on lower, warmer stretches of the same river. Hatching time is about 11:00 A.M., and the spinner fall is in the early afternoon. Hatches are usually short but heavy. A nymph fished in fast runs before and during the hatch is effective.

Epeorus longimanus nymph—
bottom view, showing
unique gills used for suction

Speckled Spinner (W)

Genus and Species	*Callibaetis coloradensis, C. nigritus*
Family	Baetadae
Emergence	June 15 to September 30
Size	8 to 10 mm (#14 and #16 hook size)
Nymph Habitat	slower rivers with aquatic vegetation

NATURAL   *ARTIFICIAL*

NYMPH

NATURAL	ARTIFICIAL
Body grayish brown	**Body** light muskrat fur
Wing Pads dark mottled brown	**Wing Pads** dark brown turkey quill segment
Tails 3, light brown	**Tails** light brown mallard
Legs light brown	**Legs** light brown mallard

DUN

NATURAL	ARTIFICIAL
Body brownish with an olive tint	**Body** medium brown and medium olive rabbit fur mixed
Wings dark gray, paths of veins and cross veins white	**Wings** slate gray hen hackle fibers, clump
Tails 2, whitish with brown at joinings	**Tails** cream hackle fibers
Legs tannish cream	**Hackle** cream, parachute

SPINNER

NATURAL	ARTIFICIAL
Body light grayish tan with tiny dark brown speckles	**Body** light gray muskrat fur
Wings hyaline, dark brown splotches on leading edge	**Wings** dark brown partridge or merganser flank fibers, spent
Tails 2, whitish with brown at joinings	**Tails** cream hackle fibers
Legs tannish cream	**Hackle** none

These mayflies are primarily lake dwellers, preferring to live among vegetation. The genus is geographically widespread over virtually all trout states from New York to California. In most areas they are only locally abundant on trout streams. Most species of *Callabaetis* are adapted to slow, warm-water situations. However, *Callabaetis coloradensis* has adapted to a colder-water environment and are found in canyons, mountains, and mountain valleys at elevations usually above 4,500 feet. In lakes, ponds, and slow-flowing rivers, nymphs are found in silted bottoms or among submerged vegetation. A closely related species, *Callibaetis nigritus,* is usually found below 5,000 feet, in valley bottoms.

The Western rivers where they are particularly important are the spring creeks. One important feature of these rivers is that they maintain a fairly constant level. There is no great runoff during the spring to scour the bottom. Vegetation, such as filamentous algae, and smooth, slow-flowing currents provide the perfect habitat for the nymphs of *Callibaetis.* Henrys Fork of the Snake is a wide, spring-creek-type river, but little over knee-deep. It emerges full blown from an underground source and is fishable when the Madison and Yellowstone are in flood stage. Its gravel bottom is carpeted with bright green aquatic vegetation.

The duns of *Callibaetis Nigritus* hatch at dusk and after dark, while those of *coloradensis* hatch at midday. They are a brownish-olive insect and have dark gray wings, with the paths of the veins and crossveins white. Adult bodies are thickly speckled with minute brown dots, set in small depressions. The fore wings of the female spinners are darkly pigmented on the leading edges. Nymphs are streamlined and fitted for swimming and darting in slow water. The spinner falls come in the morning from nine thirty to eleven and in the evening from seven to nine. The imagos sometimes fall with the smaller, but more numerous *Ephemerellas,* but the fish often prefer the larger *Callibaetis.* Rainbows from fifteen inches to eight pounds are not uncommon during this hatch and spinner fall.

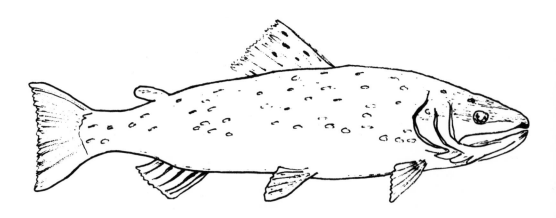

Tiny Blue-winged Olive (M, W)

Genus and Species	*Pseudocloeon anoka & Pseudocloeon edmundsi*
Family	Baetidae
Emergence	June 20 to September 30
Size	4.5 to 5 mm (#24 hook size)
Nymph Habitat	shallow gravel runs and submerged beds of vegetation

NATURAL   *ARTIFICIAL*

NYMPH

NATURAL	ARTIFICIAL
Body greenish olive, streamlined	**Body** greenish olive rabbit fur
Wing Pads brownish olive	**Wing Pads** dark brown ostrich clump
Tails 2, light olive	**Tails** light olive hackle fibers
Legs light olive	**Legs** light olive hackle fibers

DUN

NATURAL	ARTIFICIAL
Body greenish olive	**Body** greenish olive rabbit fur
Wings light gray, one pair only	**Wings** light gray hen-hackle fibers, clump
Tails 2, light gray	**Tails** light gray hackle fibers
Legs light gray	**Hackle** none or light gray parachute, 2 turns only

SPINNER

NATURAL	ARTIFICIAL
Body light olive brown with orangish cast	**Body** blend olive, light brown and orange rabbit fur
Wings hyaline	**Wings** light gray hen-hackle tips, spent
Tails 2, white	**Tails** light gray hackle fibers
Legs white	**Hackle** none

Even though these mayflies are very small in size they are extremely important to anglers in all sections of the country. They occur in great numbers, causing the fish to move out into midstream and feed freely. Pseudocloeon is multibrooded, so emergence can take place almost anytime after mid-June. However, there are two peak periods, the first occurring from late June to mid-July, and the second during late September. On dark cool days these little flies begin emerging about 11:00 A.M., continuing sporadically until dark. On warm sunny days they hatch in fantastic numbers, beginning about an hour before sundown and ending shortly after dark.

When emergence time approaches, most of the mature nymphs are found crawling on submerged vegetation. Nymphal patterns fished in these areas, or slightly downstream from weed beds, can be very deadly. As the hatch progresses, more and more fish switch to the floating duns. At this stage, a delicate #24 no-hackle dry fly is most effective. If the tails are properly split and good wing outline is maintained, these minute imitations will float upright and closely resemble the naturals on the water. The spinners normally return at dusk and are taken quietly and subtly by the trout. Sometimes close observance is required to distinguish which stage the fish are actually feeding on.

Giant Michigan Mayfly (M)

Genus and Species	*Hexagenia limbata*
Family	Ephemeridae
Other Common Names	Michigan Caddis
Emergence	June 20 to July 30
Size	18 to 33 mm (#2, #4, and #6 hook size)
Nymph Habitat	silt beds and mud banks, usually in shallow water along the streams edge

NATURAL	*ARTIFICIAL*

NYMPH

NATURAL	ARTIFICIAL
Body amber with medium brown markings	**Body** creamy tan German fitch and brown rabbit fur mixed
Wing Pads brownish black	**Wing Pads** dark brown ostrich clump
Tails 3, amber	**Tails** light tan partridge, short
Legs amber	**Legs** light tan partridge

DUN

NATURAL	ARTIFICIAL
Body varies from yellow to grayish brown, with purplish-brown back markings	**Body** natural deer body hair tied parallel to shank, ribbed with yellow tying thread
Wings smokey gray with olive reflections	**Wings** dark elk or deer body hair, clump
Tails 2, yellowish brown	**Tails** two pheasant tail fibers
Legs yellowish brown	**Hackle** brown and grizzly, parachute

SPINNER

NATURAL	ARTIFICIAL
Body yellowish with purplish-brown back markings	**Body** yellow deer body hair tied parallel to shank, ribbed with brown tying thread, regular or extended body
Wings hyaline	**Wings** double hen hackle tips, grizzly over light gray, spent
Tails 2, yellowish brown	**Tails** two long pheasant tail fibers
Legs yellowish brown	**Hackle** none

This is the famous Michigan "caddis" hatch. It is not a caddis fly, but years ago someone called it that and confusion has reigned ever since. For many anglers, these gigantic flies mark the peak of the season, especially on the larger streams such as the Pere Marquette, Au Sable, and Jordan. *Hexagenia limbata* is the Midwestern equivalent of the Eastern Green Drake hatch.

These largest of trout-stream mayflies, with their fat, meaty bodies entice large fish to feed on the surface. They hatch in tremendous numbers on warm muggy nights, beginning the second or third week in June. Peak emergence almost always comes around the Fourth of July.

Final molting to the spinner stage occurs in twenty-four to seventy-two hours, depending on the weather. The imagos normally fall from dusk to 11:00 P.M., with the females releasing their eggs in a death struggle after hitting the water. The rise form is a spectacular deep loud slurp.

In streams, the life cycle requires two years. Stomach analysis shows fish feed regularly on the nymphs during the fall and winter months. The opportunity arises when nymphs leave their burrows and swim around to molt, which occurs about thirty times as they grow. The nymphs make U-shaped holes as they burrow in the mudbanks along the edge of the stream.

Before emergence, the nymph is sometimes effective if fished just under the surface, near the silt beds where the naturals emerge. Occasionally, it will also fool a wise old feeder when every dry fly in the box has failed. Try this technique dead-drift and, if the offering is rejected, then add a slight twitch as the nymph comes into the trout's window. The addition of hackle tips to simulate partially sprouted wings is sometimes deadly.

Emergence of the duns and the return of the spinners usually take place at dusk or well after dark, and on some nights occur after midnight. Occasionally the subimagos will hatch sporadically throughout the day and the imagos will fall an hour or two before dark. This happens frequently on Michigan's Manistee River and results in some fantastic big-fly fishing during daylight hours. The fish become highly selective under these conditions, and realistic patterns are a necessity. These experiences indicate that parachute hackle and clump wings are most effective when simulating the large flies.

The double-hen-wing spinner imitation is the most deadly and realistic pattern we've developed, and it has the added advantages of floating well and being very durable. The grizzly tips simulate the dark wing markings while the light gray tips tone down the grizzly and provide the general coloration and appearance of spent wings in the film. Another effective yet simple-to-tie pattern consists of a yellow and brown fur body with gray and grizzly hackle, clipped top and bottom, for wings. The only drawback is poor flotation which results from the weight of a large hook and too little hackle. Lightweight, short-shank hooks and extended quill bodies improve buoyancy only slightly, and they have the added disadvantage of being brittle.

One fly that deserves mention for use on the *Hexagenia* hatch, is the extended-body, impala-wing fly. This fly is especially effective after dark, toward the end of the spinner fall. It is hackleless, floats low in the water and will produce as well with movement as without. This pattern has an extended body of natural deer body hair coming off a lightweight short-shank hook. Two pheasant-tail fibers protrude beyond the body to form the tails. Light gray impala is used for the spent wings, and tan mohlon, a synthetic yarn, is wrapped around the wings to form an enlarged thorax. The mohlon thorax not only creates a realistic silhouette, but also adds greatly to the flotation of the fly.

Slate-winged Olive (W)

Genus and Species	*Ephemerella flavilinea*
Family	Ephemerellidae
Emergence	June 25 to August 20
Size	8 to 10 mm (#14 and #16 hook size)
Nymph Habitat	gravel runs, medium to fast water

NATURAL	*ARTIFICIAL*

NYMPH

Body dark brown	**Body** dark blackish brown mole fur
Wing Pads black	**Wing Pads** black quill segment
Tails 3, dark brown with black bands	**Tails** dark brown partridge
Legs dark brown	**Legs** dark brown partridge

DUN

Body medium greenish olive	**Body** medium greenish olive rabbit fur
Wings dark slate	**Wing** dark gray elk hair, clump
Tails 3, dark olive gray	**Tails** dark olive hackle fibers
Legs light olive shading to brown	**Hackle** olive, parachute

SPINNER

Body light translucent reddish brown	**Body** reddish-brown buffalo fur
Wings hyaline	**Wings** light gray hen-hackle tips, spent
Tails 3, brown with dark joinings	**Tails** brown hackle fibers
Legs brown shading to dark brown	**Hackle** none

The Western Slate Olive Dun is a fly very closely resembling and immediately following the Green Drake hatch. The dun is almost indistinguishable in appearance from *Ephemerella grandis* except that it is smaller. Even so, it is still a good-sized juicy mayfly, and fine fish are attracted to it. The hatch lasts a long time, almost two months, so it is extremely important. The duns usually emerge from about 5:00 to 6:30 P.M. until dark, but on dark cloudy days we have seen them hatching all day beginning at 11:00 A.M. The spinner fall is usually in the morning from about 9:00 A.M. until 1:00 P.M., however, some spinners also fall in the evening. *Ephemerella flavilinea* and *Ephemerella grandis* belong to the same subspecies, along with *E. lata* of the Midwest, the nymphs similar in color and shape. A weighted nymph fished in the deep runs is often successful before the hatch. Emergence from the nymphal shuck takes place on the surface. We have noticed that these flies often have trouble getting one wing out of the shuck, and flounder around on the water while emerging. Thus the artificial, if given a little action, will get fish to move from their feeding lanes to take a fly acting in this manner. These insects start hatching just about the time

Ephemerella grandis, or Western Green Drake, is about finished and again the hatch comes when most Western streams are high with spring run-off water. Anglers who prefer to fish to rising trout tend to seek out water such as the large and small spring creeks and high meadow streams that do not get these floods. Therefore we run into these flies that fishermen on only the large runoff rivers, such as the Madison and the Big Hole, do not encounter. These hatches are present on the "free stone streams," but these streams are usually too dark to allow the trout to feed on the surface. A brown-bodied hen spinner is killing in the morning after a hatch the previous evening. All our dun patterns are effective during an emergence and it is well to be prepared with two or three different types, so when you miss a strike, a slightly different style can be substituted. Often the change of flies will result in a fine fish.

CHAPTER 9

The Late Season

As WE HAVE SEEN, the midseason is characterized by two radically different types of angling: evening fishing with very large flies and early-morning fishing with relatively small flies. During this time there are normally two pleasant periods each day: first when the water is warmed by the morning sun, and then, after the heat of midday, when the water cools in the evening. However, as the late season begins around the middle of July, the night hatches fade, while the morning hatches increase their intensity and longevity. By this time the heat of summer is at its peak, causing high evening water temperatures. Here again, the "pleasant time of day" rule seems to apply, as the hatches occur in the early morning when the water is at a comfortable temperature. This period shifts to midday in September, and then moves to the afternoon as the weather gets slowly colder during late fall. As the season ends the cycle is complete, with hatches coming at the same time they did when the season opened.

This season, to us, is the most interesting of all, and the most challenging. The naturals are very small, mostly in the 3.5- to 5-mm range, making light, delicate equipment the order of the day. We use #4 rods and lines, combined with size #22 to #28 flies and 6X to 7X leaders. Hatches of these tiny flies are very dependable, much more so than the larger species. Good fish feed with extreme regularity and must rise more times to get a full meal. They seem to lose much of their natural caution: in fact, it is sometimes difficult to put them down, especially at the peak of the hatch, when they are gorging heavily.

The fish, however, are very selective, and correct imitations are a must if you are to be at all successful. Contrary to popular opinion, just any small fly will not work well. A 5-mm imitation of a *Tricorythodes* dun, when the natural is only 3.5 mm long, is useless. The difference between a #22 and #28 does not appear great, but relatively, it is over 40 percent, and the fish can easily recognize the disparity. When fishing to these small flies, you should carry a millimeter gauge and measure the naturals.

The major difficulty with small standard imitations is that too much hackle is used and it is usually too long. Hackle on these flies only obscures, or completely obliterates, the delicate outline of the insect and gives the impression of a fuzzy dandelion seed.

For years we incorrectly blamed the small hooks for not holding well. Only one or two fish out of ten might be landed. However, we found that when we follow these rules, #28s are just as efficient as #14s.

(1) The fly must be the right size, color, and silhouette.

(2) The fly must float and behave in the same manner as the natural. Generally, for freshly hatched duns and newly fallen spinners, imitations must float high in the film and not be waterlogged. To accomplish this, saturate the fly with a waterproofing agent, and then, after drying completely, add either a more viscous liquid floatant, such as silicone, or rub in a paste dressing. The first step prevents waterlogging, while the latter provides the film necessary for proper flotation.

(3) The hook must be offset slightly, especially for sizes #20 to #28.

When we started following these rules we landed many more fish and, in fact, had trouble unhooking them. We now use barbless hooks, which hold just as well as regular hooks and permit release without injury. This ease of unhooking not only protects the trout but also preserves delicate dry flies. An even further advantage is that more valuable fishing time is gained. Time that would normally be utilized for unhooking barbed flies and changing crushed, slimy dressings, can be spent more profitably during the all-too-short hatch period.

If everyone knew how enjoyable the late season was, it might lose one of its sweetest charms—solitude. Gone are the hordes of Opening Week, gone are the multitudes, who line the banks at every good hole, reserving them for the night hatches of *Hexagenia limbata* or *Ephemera simulans*. The majority of anglers hang up their rods after the large flies are done for the season, and consequently we find beautiful runs deserted, day-hatching mayflies, free-rising trout, and pleasant weather. To pick only one season, this is it. To us, a fifteen-inch brown on a #28 and 7X is far more thrilling than a twenty-four incher on heavier tackle.

Yellow May, Yellow Drake (E)

Genus and Species	*Ephemera varia*
Family	Ephemeridae
Emergence	June 25 to July 25
Size	13 to 16 mm (#10 and #12 hook size)
Nymph Habitat	in a mixture of sand and gravel, also in silt and mudbanks

NATURAL	ARTIFICIAL

NYMPH

NATURAL	ARTIFICIAL
Body amber with dark brown markings	**Body** creamy tan German fitch and brown rabbit fur mixed
Wing Pads dark brown	**Wing Pads** dark brown ostrich, clump
Tails 3, amber	**Tails** light tan partridge, short
Legs amber	**Legs** light tan partridge

DUN

NATURAL	ARTIFICIAL
Body pale yellow, brown markings on back	**Body** deer body hair tinted yellow, yellow thread ribbing
Wings light yellowish-gray, spotted with brown	**Wings** clump of light deer body hair, tinted yellow
Tails 3, yellow mottled with brown	**Tails** light ginger hackle fibers
Legs yellow, brown markings on forelegs	**Hackle** light ginger and grizzly, parachute

SPINNER

NATURAL	ARTIFICIAL
Body pale yellowish-olive with brown markings on back	**Body** pale yellow and light olive rabbit fur mixed
Wings hyaline spotted with dark brownish-black	**Wings** grizzly hen hackle tips, spent
Tails 3, yellow mottled with brown	**Tails** light ginger hackle fibers
Legs yellow, brownish markings on forelegs	**Hackle** bronze blue dun, sparse and undersize

The nymphs of *Ephemera varia* possesses many of the same characteristics as those of *Ephemera guttulata,* such as flanged legs, tusks, feathery gills, and rapid emergence. However, they can be differentiated from the Green Drake nymphs by their smaller size, darker coloration and distinctive markings both dorsally and ventrally. The underside of the abdomen displays blackish longitudinal markings while the back of the entire body exhibits a unique pattern. This aesthetic dorsal design is a deep chocolate brown in coloration and is discernible in both the subimago and imago stages.

Emergence normally occurs at twilight, but when the weather is cloudy and cool the duns can be seen sporadically all day. Their beautiful color and large size make a very impressive sight, especially when either duns or spinners appear in any great quantity. Adults usually return to the stream the day after emergence and begin their mating flight at dusk.

Slate-winged Olive (M)

Genus and Species *Ephemerella lata*
Family Ephemerellidae
Emergence July 1 to August 10
Size 6 to 9 mm (#16 or #18 hook size)
Nymph Habitat gravel riffles in streams of all sizes

NATURAL	ARTIFICIAL

NYMPH

Body Brownish black, robust	**Body** dark Belgian mole fur
Wing Pads brownish black	**Wing Pads** black crow-quill segment
Tails 3, brown	**Tails** brown partridge
Legs brownish black	**Legs** dark brown partridge

DUN

Body olive	**Body** olive rabbit fur
Wings dark gray, almost black	**Wings** dark gray turkey breast, clump
Tails 3, olive	**Tails** olive hackle fibers
Legs olive	**Hackle** olive, parachute

SPINNER

Body males brown, females light olive	**Body** medium brown or light olive rabbit fur
Wings hyaline	**Wings** light gray hen-hackle tips, spent
Tails 3, light olive	**Tails** light olive hackle fibers
Legs light olive	**Hackle** none

Ephemerella lata is one of the first good early-morning hatches of the season. Emergence can begin as early as 6:30 A.M. and continue until noon with the peak period occurring from 7:00 to 9:00 A.M. The duns appear sporadically over an extended period, rarely hatching with any considerable concentrations at a given time. Often they are on the water simultaneously with other more numerous species, such as *Pseudocloeon anoka* and *Tricorythodes stygiatus*, causing the fish to ignore them completely. However, there is a period in mid-July when *Pseudocloeon* is fading and *Tricorythodes* is barely existent that provides excellent early-morning activity.

The nymphal imitation is sometimes effective before any surface activity is noticed. It should be fished along the bottom of gravel riffles with an occasional twitch. As the hatch commences, an emerging pattern is deadly floating in the film dead-drift. The emerging pattern is the same as the nymphal imitation, except that dark grayish-black points are used in place of wing pads. These emergent wings should be three-quarters the body length and tied back at a 45° angle. The suggested pattern for the subimago can be tied without hackle as long as the tails are split properly.

The spinners of *Ephemerella lata* return just before sundown, and fall for almost an hour after dark, providing tremendous evening fishing. In the

Midwest, this is the last hatch of good-sized flies of the season and the fish seem to know it. After these juicy morsels leave the water, most of the good hatches are size #20 or smaller. The spinners are far more important than the duns for two reasons. First, the duns hatch sporadically over a four or five-hour period in the morning, resulting in a low-intensity emergence and slow feeding activity; then the following evening, the same number of flies return as spinners and fall en masse in about ninety minutes, causing frenzied activity. Second, the duns must compete with other more numerous species in the morning, while the spinners have little or no competition in the evening.

Pale Morning Dun #2 (W)

Genus and Species	*Ephremerella inermis*
Family	Ephemerellidae
Other Common Names	Olive Quill
Emergence	July 1 to August 30
Size	5.5 to 7 mm (#20 and #22 hook size)
Nymph Habitat	gravel and aquatic vegetation, all speeds of water

NATURAL	ARTIFICIAL

NYMPH

NATURAL	ARTIFICIAL
Body dark brownish olive	**Body** dark brown and medium olive rabbit fur mixed
Wing Pads dark olive brown	**Wing Pads** olive brown duck quill segment
Tails 3, brown with black bands	**Tails** dark brown partridge or merganser flank fibers
Legs brownish olive	**Legs** dark brown partridge or merganser flank fibers

DUN

NATURAL	ARTIFICIAL
Body bright, light olive yellow	**Body** light olive and light yellow rabbit fur mixed
Wings light gray	**Wings** light gray hen-hackle fibers, clump
Tails 3, tan with dark brown at joinings	**Tails** bronze blue-dun hackle fibers
Legs light olive	**Hackle** light olive, parachute

SPINNER

NATURAL	ARTIFICIAL
Body male yellowish brown, female yellowish olive	**Body** mix either dark brown or light olive with yellow rabbit fur
Wings hyaline	**Wings** medium gray hackle, clipped on bottom
Tails 3, light tan with brown joinings	**Tails** bronze blue-dun hackle fibers
Legs olive tan	**Hackle** none

Ephemerella inermis is the most widespread and numerous of the Western *Ephemerellas* and is characterized by a beautiful but elusive olive-yellow cast. The fish become extremely selective during this hatch and an artificial, either too large or off color, is usually ignored. The fly resembles the Eastern *Ephemerella dorothea* but is a trifle smaller and more olive. The spinner fall is at 9:30 A.M. on Henrys Fork of the Snake in Idaho and they literally carpet the water for about two hours. The duns start emerging around 11:00 A.M. and continue all afternoon. At about 6:00 P.M. the spinner fall starts again and lasts until dusk. Trout rise all day to this hatch and rainbows up to eight pounds can be taken on #20 dry flies. Often there are so many naturals on the water that you must cast your artificial to fit in with the feeding rhythm of the fish. Otherwise it will drift along untouched with hundreds of the naturals.

Before we fished Henrys Fork of the Snake, we would never have believed so many mayflies could hatch in such great numbers so steadily, for many hours each day for two months. Even more amazing is the fact that great hatches of *Tricorythodes, Pseudocloeon, Callibaetis, Baetis,* and two other species of *Ephemerellas* are hatching simultaneously. This very large spring creek is the most prolific insect factory we have ever seen.

The dun is best imitated by a #20 or #22 hen-hackle fiber wing, chartreuse fur body, and sparse parachute hackle. Other patterns equally as effective are the duck-shoulder and duck-quill-segment type with no hackle. A killing pattern for the spinner is an olive yellow fur body tied with full medium gray hackle and then clipped only on the bottom. A small dark brown nymph is deadly just before and during the early part of the hatch.

Tiny White-winged Black (E, M, W)

Genus and Species	*Tricorythodes* (Various species)
Family	Caenidae
Emergence	July 1 to September 30
Size	3 to 6 mm (#20 to #28 hook size)
Nymph Habitat	quiet water where silt and debris collect

NATURAL   *ARTIFICIAL*

NYMPH

NATURAL	ARTIFICIAL
Body dark brown with light rings in abdomen	**Body** dark brown rabbit fur, thick at thorax
Wing Pads blackish brown	**Wing Pads** dark Belgian mole clump
Tails 3, tannish	**Tails** tan hen-hackle fibers
Legs tannish	**Legs** tan hen-hackle fiber

DUN

NATURAL	ARTIFICIAL
Body brownish black, robust thorax	**Body** brownish black mole fur, heavy at thorax
Wings whitish	**Wings** light gray hen hackle fibers, clump
Tails 3, whitish	**Tails** light gray hackle fibers
Legs whitish	**Hackle** none

SPINNER

NATURAL	ARTIFICIAL
Body brownish black, robust thorax	**Body** brownish black mole fur, heavy at thorax
Wings hyaline whitish	**Wings** light gray hen-hackle tips, spent
Tails 3, whitish, four times body length	**Tails** long light gray hackle fibers
Legs reddish brown fading to white	**Hackle** none

Few anglers are familiar with these extremely small but important mayflies. This is probably due to the fact that they come after the larger, well-known hatches are over and also due to the time of hatching activity. Emergence takes place during the morning hours, normally between 5:00 add 7:00 A.M., somewhat later on Western streams, with mating flights forming almost immediately. Final molting actually takes place in the air shortly after the duns have emerged. Subimaginal skins, shed in this manner, can be observed falling to the water and floating downstream. These integuments, whitish in appearance, are a welcome sight to the angler. Their presence is a good indication that the spinners will be on the water shortly.

The nymphs of *Tricorythodes* are easily recognized by the enlarged triangular gill plates of the second adbominal segment and by the long slender hairs that cover the body, legs, and tails. The hair collects trash and debris which can be seen clinging to the various parts of the body. Nymphal patterns are sometimes effective at the beginning of the hatch, and they should be fished in the film dead-drift. The fish, however, seem to prefer the winged stages, especially the spinners. This preference is undoubtedly due to the fact that the imagos return to the water in such fantastic numbers.

When the emergence is well under way, imitations of the freshly hatched duns should be used, at least until the first spinners begin to fall. A clump of light gray hen-hackle fibers makes an excellent wing outline and is very durable. Turkey-breast and duck-shoulder feathers, in the proper color, can also be used effectively.

Soon after the first spinners begin to fall, a point is reached where some fish are still feeding on the duns while others have switched over to the spent variety. Sometimes they all seem to switch at once, but at other times, individuals show distinct preferences. These situations require close observation to determine which pattern should be used. Eventually, however, the imagos dominate completely and the spinner pattern becomes a must. By this time, fish of all sizes have moved into their feeding positions, and are rising eagerly. During this period, the fish also become extremely selective, thus creating a situation where it is imperative to have the *right fly*.

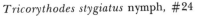
Tricorythodes stygiatus nymph, #24

The suggested spinner pattern, utilizing hen-hackle points for the wings, is normally very deadly, but there are occasions when a hackled fly is preferred. Substitute light gray or bronze blue-dun hackle for the hen points. Keep the wing outline sparse and delicate by using no more than two or three turns of hackle. Some species have a lighter abdomen, either whitish or light olive, a feature that can be incorporated to give more realism. Probably the most important requirement for these small flies is to maintain realistic dimensions. *Tricorythodes stygiatus* requires a #28 or #24 hook size (#28 is best); a #22 will be completely ignored. As a double check on size, put the natural and artificial side by side for comparison. For the angler equipped with the right pattern in the right size, this hatch provides the ultimate in small-fly, fine-tackle fishing.

Slate-cream Dun (W)

Genus and Species	*Epeorus albertae*
Family	Baetidae
Size	9 to 10 mm (#14 or #16 hook size)
Emergence	July 5 to August 15
Nymph Habitat	medium to fast gravel runs

NATURAL   *ARTIFICIAL*

NYMPH

Natural	Artificial
Body gray with brown markings	**Body** brownish gray muskrat fur
Wing Pads dark gray	**Wing Pads** dark gray quill segment
Tails 2, gray with brown markings	**Tails** light partridge
Legs gray with brown markings	**Legs** light partridge

DUN

Natural	Artificial
Body grayish pink with brown markings on back	**Body** light gray and pink rabbit fur mixed
Wings medium gray	**Wing Pads** medium gray duck shoulder feathers
Tails 2, ginger	**Tails** ginger hackle fibers
Legs cream with tan markings	**Hackle** none or medium gray v hackle

SPINNER

Natural	Artificial
Body cream to light grayish tan	**Body** light grayish tan beaver or rabbit fur
Wings hyaline	**Wings** light gray hen-hackle tips, spent
Tails 2, brown	**Tails** brown hackle fibers
Legs brown	**Hackle** none

This small cream mayfly is widely distributed over the West. It occurs in the lower, warmer stretches of streams and gradually replaces *E. longimanus* which is found in the upper, colder stretches. The spinner fall is early morning and late evening. Emergence is at twilight. Nymphs are found in fast water and the adult duns emerge underwater, making a small light-color wet fly a killing pattern during the hatch. The underside of the duns sometimes has a distinct pinkish cast.

Two other species of *Epeorus, E. grandis* and *E. deceptivus*, are less common but are present in the West. *E. grandis* is a large species found in small, fast streams above 5,000 feet with a daytime temperature of 45° or lower. It hatches in early June, July and early August. *E. deceptivus* is similar to *E. longimanus*, 8 to 9 mm long, and the spinner is light brown.

Pale Morning Dun #3 (W)

Genus and Species	*Ephemerella infrequens*
Family	Ephemerellidae
Emergence	July 15 to October 30
Size	7 to 9 mm (#16 and #18 hook size)
Nymph Habitat	under rocks and gravel in moderate to slow currents

NATURAL	ARTIFICIAL

NYMPH

NATURAL	ARTIFICIAL
Body medium brown	**Body** medium brown fur
Wing Pads dark brown	**Wing Pads** dark brown ostrich clump
Tails 3, tan, mottled with dark brown	**Tails** dark brown partridge
Legs tan, mottled with dark brown	**Legs** dark brown partridge

DUN

NATURAL	ARTIFICIAL
Body yellowish with distinct olive cast	**Body** pale yellow and light olive rabbit fur mixed
Wings light yellowish gray	**Wings** light gray duck shoulder, tinted yellow
Tails 3, light olive	**Tails** light olive hackle fibers
Legs light olive	**Hackle** none or sparse light olive v hackle

SPINNER

NATURAL	ARTIFICIAL
Body chocolate brown with yellowish cast	**Body** reddish brown and yellow fur
Wings hyaline	**Wings** bronze blue-dun hackle
Tails 3, light tan	**Tails** bronze blue-dun hackle fibers
Legs tan, forelegs brown	**Hackle** none

Ephemerella infrequens is undoubtedly one of the most important and prolific hatches in the West. It is a fairly large fly and emerges in fantastic numbers, two factors which combine to provide an enormous food supply for the trout. It also hatches over a longer period of time, staying on the water for a major portion of the season. With all of these available meals floating by their noses, the fish automatically become highly selective.

Another factor that contributes greatly to this selectivity is the elusive coloration of the duns. To the naked eye, the body color appears to be a cream or pale yellow shade. In fact, most of the local fly shops have row after row of cream and yellow-bodied flies, most of which are ineffective when floated over selective trout.

After experiencing the same frustrations as everyone else, we discovered through our close-up photographs that the subimaginal body has shades of both yellow and olive, while the wing is light gray tinted with yellow. This information, incorporated into a no-hackle-type fly, resulted in some very effective patterns. The listed pattern has wings fashioned from light gray duck-shoulder feathers that have been tinted with yellow. Great pains should be taken to select feathers with plenty of body—ones that will hold their shape when wet. Even the highest quality feathers will slim down in water, so it is advisable to begin with a broader outline than displayed by the natural.

Two other wing variations that have also proven their effectiveness on finicky risers should be mentioned. One is a matched pair of duck-quill segments dyed to the proper yellowish gray shade. These actually appear the most realistic, but are not as durable. It is recommended that these be used without hackle, though sparse light olive V hackle can be added if preferred. The other variation is a clump of yellowish gray turkey-breast fibers with a couple turns of light olive hackle, parachute style. The body used with all wing variations is the same, a mixture of pale yellow and light olive fur.

As hatch time approaches, the nymphs of *infrequens* get very active on the stream bottom. This situation provides excellent action if sinking lines and weighted artificials are used. Imitations must be twitched right on the bottom to be effective. Even after the hatch is in full progress, many fish can be observed snatching up nymphs before they can make their rapid dash to the surface. Nymphing in this manner, though certainly effective, is not very enjoyable.

As the hatch progresses, most of the fish become surface oriented and commence feeding on flies that are drifting or swimming in close proximity to the water's surface. This situation gives rise to the possibility of at least three patterns which could be used to imitate the various stages in the hatching process. The first would be an emerging pattern, devised to simulate the nymph as its wings unfold from the wing case. This stage takes

Ephemerella infrequens
nymph, #16

place as the natural swims within a few inches of the waters surface. The required pattern is the same as suggested for the nymph, except that the wing pads are replaced with medium-gray hackle points tied short.

After their nymphal cases have been shed, it is common for many of the duns to drift along slightly awash, trying to dry their bedraggled wings. This condition creates the need for a second emerging-type pattern similar to the suggested dun imitation; however, the duck-shoulder feathers should be tied short and the pattern should be pulled into the film to form a low silhouette. The third pattern, of course, is an imitation of the fully emerged dun that is floating on the surface with upright wings.

The hatch usually begins around 11:00 A.M. with peak emergence coming between noon and 2:00 P.M. Depending on weather conditions, sporadic activity can occur all afternoon and into the early evening hours. Feeding intensity tapers off greatly during this later period, but often a real lunker can be found sipping gently and subtly.

We have yet to experience a heavy spinner fall of this species. On several occasions, however, sporadic mating flights have been observed from late afternoon until twilight, causing sparse feeding activity.

Slate-gray Dun (W)

Genus and Species	*Heptagenia elegantula*
Family	Heptageniidae
Emergence	August 5 to September 25
Size	9 to 10 mm (#14 or #16 hook size)
Nymph Habitat	warmer silted streams below 6,000 feet

NATURAL	ARTIFICIAL
NYMPH	
Body grayish brown	**Body** grayish-brown muskrat or rabbit fur
Wing Pads dark gray	**Wing Pads** dark gray quill segment
Tails 3, gray, banded	**Tails** dark partridge fibers
Legs gray with dark markings	**Legs** dark partridge fibers
DUN	
Body grayish olive with brown bands	**Body** light gray and olive rabbit fur mixed, ribbed with brown thread
Wings dark gray	**Wings** dark gray duck-shoulder feathers
Tails 2, gray	**Tails** gray hackle fibers
Legs tannish shading to brown	**Hackle** none
SPINNER	
Body brownish yellow	**Body** medium brown and yellow rabbit fur mixed
Wings hyaline	**Wings** light gray hen-hackle tips, spent
Tails 2, dark gray	**Tails** dark gray hackle fibers
Legs dark gray	**Hackle** none

This delicate little species is very prevalent over the West, and important on many rivers. The spinner fall is in the evening, but emergence takes place about eleven in the morning. Although the duns often emerge in great numbers, emergence usually does not last long. In general, various *Heptagenia* species, though rare in the Midwest, are common in the West. The sizes of the numerous species vary from 5 to 15 mm and color varies from cream to dark brown. The nymphs have three tails instead of the two that *Epeorus* nymphs have, which they otherwise resemble. Another fairly common *Heptagenia* species is *H. criddleri,* which is 7 mm long. The spinners have a light gray abdomen with dark brown lateral patches, dark brown thorax and legs, and hyaline wings.

Gray Drake (W)

Genus and Species	*Siphlonurus occidentalis*
Family	Baetidae
Emergence	August 10 to October 10
Size	12 to 15 mm (#10 and #12 hook size)
Nymph Habitat	quiet water, especially around the edges of trout streams and in back waters

NATURAL	*ARTIFICIAL*

NYMPH

Body brownish gray with dark brown markings	**Body** gray muskrat fur
Wing Pads dark brownish gray	**Wing Pads** dark brown quill section
Tails 3, tan marked with brown	**Tails** brown partridge
Legs tan marked with brown	**Legs** brown partridge

DUN

Body olive gray with dark brown markings	**Body** gray deer hair elongated body, ribbed with dark brown thread
Wings dark slate	**Wings** two partridge-breast feathers dyed dark gray
Tails 2, dark gray	**Tails** dark grey hackle fibers
Legs gray shading to dark gray brown	**Hackle** 1 short hackle tied in normally with fibers clipped top and bottom (V hackle type)

SPINNER

Body dark grayish brown with light rings	**Body** dark grayish brown muskrat fur
Wings hyaline	**Wings** light gray hen-hackle tips, spent
Tails 2, dark grayish brown	**Tails** dark brown hackle fibers
Legs dark grayish brown	**Hackle** none

This large grayish mayfly is quite common on most Western trout streams. It is found all over the Rockies from Colorado to California. The nymph is a free-swimming type with a flattened body and large head, and according to Edmunds is omnivorous, feeding on plant and insect life in slow-moving water on the stream bottom. Gray Drakes are found around 3 to 5,000 feet in streams with a daytime temperature of 45° to 65°. The spinner fall is in the midmorning and in the evening. On a cloudy day it will be found in midday. It emerges sporadically from about 11:00 A.M. until 1:00 P.M. There are few duns on the water, but the fly is so large and enticing that fish seem to be on the lookout for them. The nymph imitation is good fished with a darting motion along the edges of the stream. The Gray Drake is quite common on the Snake in Idaho, the Yellowstone, and the Madison in Wyoming and Montana.

CHAPTER 10

Caddis Flies, Stone Flies, and Midges—The Downwings

THOUGH THE MAJOR PORTION of our study is concerned with mayflies, or the upwings, several other groups of aquatic insects also play an important role in the feeding habits of the trout. These flies form a group we call the downwings and consists of caddis flies, stone flies, and midges. In general, mayflies represent the most significant segment of the trout's diet, but there are times when one of the downwings can change this situation. The *Chimarra* caddis, for example, is one of the season's finest hatches on Michigan's Au Sable River. Clouds of these flies are so dense at times that it's difficult to keep them out of your eyes. Often the fish will feed on the magnitude of little *Chimarras* even though large juicy Hendricksons are on the water at the same time. Another Michigan river, the Muskegon, has unusually heavy caddis-fly hatches every day of the season. Therefore, for this river at least, these flies are more important than mayflies.

Previously, one of the richest streams known to us was the North Branch of the Au Sable River where Dr. J. W. Leonard collected over twelve hundred mayfly nymphs per square foot of bottom. However, Dr. Leonard

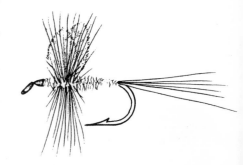

This half-spent Adams-type fly can be used to imitate flying caddis flies, stone flies, and midges

told us that one of his students collected over five thousand caddis worms per square foot of bottom on the Pigeon River, below a dam. By these facts, it is evident that caddis flies are much more important than most anglers realize. There are many species, over four hundred known in Michigan alone, making it impossible to handle them as we did the mayflies. You should familiarize yourself with the colors and sizes of caddis flies that make up the fishing hatches in your area.

The stone flies are of comparatively minor importance to Eastern and Midwestern fishing, since many species climb out of the water to hatch on logs and rocks, and thus do not produce a rise of trout. However, there are usually a few species in most areas which make up good fishing hatches for a few weeks in the year. In the West, for example, there is an extremely large stone fly known as the Salmon Fly, which provides some of the best fishing of the season. In June, when this fly is hatching on rivers such as the Yellowstone and Madison, fly-fishing for really giant trout is the order of the day.

On most streams, there are numerous periods during the year when midges form a significant portion of the trout's diet. In October, we have seen eighteen- to twenty-two-inch browns and rainbows on the Missouri River in Montana feeding on green midges. At dawn in midsummer, larger fish will often feed on these minature flies, completely ignoring the larger mayflies which are hatching simultaneously. On a sunny winter afternoon, trout in Michigan, Pennsylvania, and Montana can be seen rising to midges. Thus, this fly provides food for the fish all year long.

CADDIS FLIES

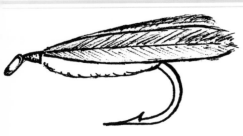

No-hackle hen caddis

No-hackle turkey caddis

The caddis flies comprise the order *Trichoptera* and in North America alone there are almost a thousand known species. Unlike mayflies, they have what is called a complete life cycle which includes egg, larva, pupa, and adult. The *Ephemeroptera* have only one stage between egg and adult, the nymph stage. Caddis larvae display a general wormlike appearance with a dark and somewhat hairy head. Behind the head are three thoracic elements—pronotum, mesonotum, and metanotum—followed by ten abdominal segments. Short threadlike gills are normally located along the abdomen and small legs or hooks extend from the rear of the body for the purpose of securing the larva to its case or another object.

Numerous types of larval forms exist and each is unique. The free-living form neither builds a shelter nor has a case and are completely free to move about in flowing water. Another form, called the net spinners, build variously shaped netlike shelters and attach them to plants, weeds, or other underwater supports. These webby structures are spun from silk and are used to trap food and debris. The larva keeps its head close to the net and seizes any edible materials that become trapped. Other types form tubular-shaped structures by digging into sand bottoms and then cementing the burrow into a firm shelter. The greatest majority of caddis-fly larvae, known as the casemakers, construct portable shelters which can be dragged with them as they move about. They construct a great variety of cases out of such

Caddis in case, from underwater

Caddis worm

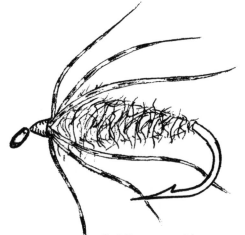

Caddis pupa, with sparse partridge collar

Caddis pupa—duck-shoulder
wings, with partridge legs

Caddis pupa with heavier
partridge collar—fur heavily
picked to create fat body

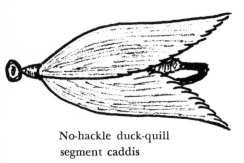

No-hackle duck-quill
segment caddis

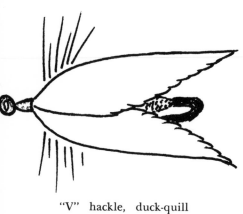

"V" hackle, duck-quill
segment caddis

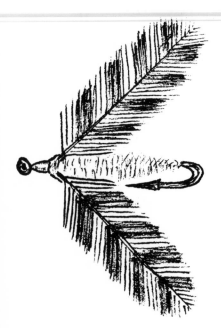

No-hackle, grizzly hen,
spent caddis

materials as twigs, leaves, stones, sand, and shells which are bonded or cemented with silk. A few species utilize the silk-spinning process to make complete cases.

When pupation begins, the free-living larvae types form a cocoonlike pupal cell, while the casemaking variety merely seals off the open end and pupates in the case. During this stage, the pupa develops wing cases, a heavy thorax, long legs, and does not eat. Emergence, in most species, is accomplished when the pupa tears out of its case, swims actively to the surface, sheds its pupal covering and immediately takes to the air as a moth-like adult. Fantastic fishing can be had at this time if a good pupal imitation is used to simulate the free-swimming natural. In some species, the pupa crawls out on a stone or log to shed its skin, thus eliminating the effective usage of the pupal pattern.

Adult caddis flies have two pairs of wings which are held over the body in a tent or rooflike manner and are hairy in texture. They are normally dull or somber colored and have long slender antennae. Caddis flies live longer than mayflies, as they have a method of absorbing liquid foods. This counteracts loss of moisture, which is a senior factor in insect longevity. Under natural conditions, a week to ten days would be the normal life-span of an adult caddis. The flies mate while at rest and the females fly away to lay their eggs. Some species oviposit on the surface, some dive beneath the water and attach their eggs to underwater objects, and others lay their eggs on vegetation bordering or overhanging the water. The first two methods are more important to fishermen.

Hatches of caddis flies are generally less concentrated and more drawn out over the season than mayflies. Notable exceptions are some of the early season *Chimarras* known as the Little Black caddis. This fly hatches about the same time as the Hendrickson and lasts two to three weeks. The *Chimarras* are in the #16 to #18 size range and appear around noon, about two hours before the larger mayflies. When the Hendrickson hatch is over, about 4:00 P.M., the female caddis lay their eggs which are formed into a very conspicuous green sac. At this point, the trout switch from Hendrickson duns to *Chimarra* spinners, but a little later they switch again to Hendrickson spinners. You must be alert to which stage of which insect the trout are feeding on, and change with them. From noon until dusk, there is a continuous rise of trout to one stage or the other of the two different insects, which makes this a truly great part of the fishing season.

Anglers seem to have difficulty recognizing when a caddis hatch is in progress. This may be due to the peculiarity of adults taking to the air immediately on shedding the pupal husk. These freshly hatched flies do not float along drying their wings as most mayflies do, so are seldom seen on the water. The pupas are almost impossible to detect, as they are either flush in the film or underwater, making their mad dash toward the surface. Usually, two factors help to determine when an emergence of caddis flies is taking place: adult flies will be seen in the air and trout will be bulging to the swift-moving pupas.

One important aspect of fishing adult patterns is to determine whether the fish are taking flies that are *at rest,* moving *on* the water, or flying *over* the water. If the preferred naturals are drifting motionless, then a sparsely hackled, low-silhouette, downwing pattern fished dead-drift is required. Imitation of on-water movement is best accomplished with a higher riding downwing and a greased leader coordinated with the proper rod movements. Flying caddis are best·imitated with body-matching, Adams-type flies which should be used to hit a fish "right on the head" as quickly as possible after detecting a rise.

Shaped-wing "V" hackle caddis

STONE FLIES

The stone flies make up one of the smaller orders of aquatic insects, yet there are approximately four hundred species existing in North America. This order, known as Plecoptera, consists of two suborders: Setipalpia, in which the nymphs are normally carnivorous, and Filipalpia, which includes species that are mainly vegetarians. In general, Filipalpia nymphs are more abundant in colder streams and feed primarily on plant life, while the Setipalpia are more commonly located in warmer water and feed on smaller insects.

Probably the easiest way to distinguish stone-fly from mayfly nymphs is to remember that most of the stone fly's features appear in pairs. They have two relatively long antennae and two bristlelike tails, with both antennae and tails about equal in length. Twin pairs of evenly proportioned wing cases appear over the thoracic area and at the termination of each leg are located a pair of tarsal claws. Other identifying features include the presence of either two or three ocelli and three tarsal segments on each leg. Gills are filiform, or threadlike, and can be located in a variety of areas, in-

Yellow stone-fly nymph, #16

cluding the thorax, abdomen, neck, chin, or anal regions. In general, the nymphal stage exists for one year but can last as long as two or three years for some species. Most stone-fly nymphs emerge by crawling out of the water onto an object such as a large stone and shedding their skin. A few species, however, emerge on the surface and float for a long time rather than taking to the air instantly like the caddis fly.

Adult stone flies have two pairs of wings which exhibit primitive venation and are held over the body in a flat position when the insect is at rest. In flight, they are awkward compared to the grace of the mayfly, and both pairs of wings show up distinctly as they wing their way slowly over the water. Two tails and the flat position of the wings help differentiate the stone fly from the adult caddis, which lacks tails and holds its wing in a rooflike position. The life-span of the adult stone fly is about two to three weeks, during which they are inactive and hide in dark sheltered areas to take nourishment. Egg laying occurs on the surface, either while flying over the water, dipping down to it, or while swimming, usually across and upstream. During this time, a fly fished in a like manner is quite effective.

Stone fly at rest—groundhog wings, "V" hackle

Patterns and techniques, used when adult stone flies are on the water, compare rather closely to the types of dressing and procedures required for adult caddis flies. Downwing sparsely hackled flies, floated dead drift, are in order when the naturals are motionless, while the Adams-type imitations can be very effective when motion must be simulated. Some of the larger stone flies, thirty to fifty millimeters in length, are nocturnal and their imitation is best accomplished with hair-wing, mohlon-body-type patterns.

MIDGES

The order Diptera is made up of a large and divergent group of aquatic insects more popularly called midges, flies, mosquitoes, and gnats. Of this group, the midges are most important to the fly-fisherman. These so-called nonbiting midges constitute the family Tendipedidae which, by themselves, create an extremely significant segment in the ecology of aquatic environment. Not only do midges play an important role in the diet of the trout, but they are also preyed upon by other insects. Midges are more abundant in streams containing heavy plant growth and prefer soft silt and muck bottoms to sand and gravel. They can survive in a wide range of habitats and temperatures.

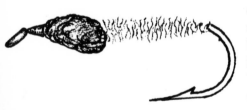

Midge pupa with fur case

The life cycle of midges, consisting of egg, larva, pupa, and adult, is complete. The larvae are wormlike in appearance, vary greatly in coloration, and many are less than one-eighth of an inch in length. Some species are predaceous, mainly on other larvae, while others feed on detritus and plankton. Pupation can occur inside the last larval skin or, in some species, can take place inside a silk cocoon, or gelatinous case. The pupa features a slender delicate abdomen, a slightly enlarged thorax, and wing pads that hang close to the underside of the body. Just before emergence, the pupae migrate to the surface of the water, where they hang vertically in the film, drifting on the current. Pupal imitations fished in a like manner can be deadly during this period. Dressings are simple but must normally be tied

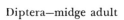

Midge larva

Diptera—midge adult

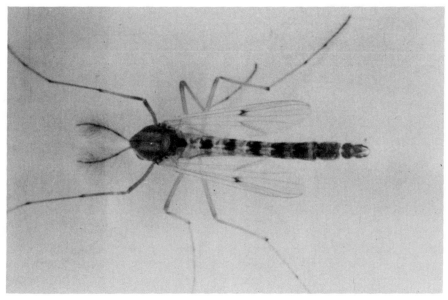

No-hackle midge at rest—hen
hackle fiber wings

Hen midge, "V" hackle type

on extremely small hooks; sometimes #28s are not minute enough. These patterns should be fished dead drift, utilizing long fine leaders.

Midge adults have only one pair of wings and can be found in a wide variety of colors. There are so many combinations of colors that it's almost impossible to be equipped with the proper pattern at all times. It is wise, however, to tie up a number of size #22s, #24s and #28s in several shades ranging from dark to light. Normally, size is more critical with these small flies than exact color or pattern. If a more realistic imitation is required, the portable streamside kit can be put to use. Midge dressings are quite simple to fashion, so minimum fishing time will be sacrificed utilizing the vise. Another favorable factor is the relative longevity of midge hatches. If an effective pattern is not available, it's always the best policy to catch a sample and start tying.

Normally, when fishing midges, the pupal imitation is far more effective than the adult pattern. This is due to the fact that the pupas drift in the film for relatively long periods of time, often in extremely large numbers. When the adults emerge, they quickly shed their pupal skin and take immediately to the air. Once airborne, they fly low *over* the water's surface, but rarely land on it. Small trout will occasionally take the low-flying adults, but most of the fish will feed exclusively on the pupal stage. The important thing to remember is that the pupas are *in* the water, where they are *easily available* to the trout, while the adults are *out* of the water, making them *less available* to the trout.

Always carry some of these small patterns, no matter where you fish. These "little bits of hair and hackle" have saved the day on numerous trips. We can recall many memorable instances, on such rivers as the Battenkill, Paradise Creek, Musconetcong, Beaverkill, and Paulinskill when midges provided excellent angling. Even in Montana, where everyone mistakenly thinks in terms of large flies, the gray-winged olive-bodied midge has furnished tremendous late-season fishing. In Michigan, there are several mid- to late-summer periods when the emergence of midges is the feature hatch of the day. Nothing is more challenging than trying for good-sized fish that are feeding on midges at midday. Taking these fish in the eighteen- to twenty-inch class on #28 flies and 7X tippets is a thrill long remembered.

Midge pupa with duck-shoulder case

CHAPTER 11

Terrestrials

THE FLIES THAT we have designated as the upwings and the downwings comprise the major portion of the trout's diet during the greater part of the season. On most streams, mayflies provide the greatest volume of food, followed by caddis flies, stone flies, and midges, in that order. At certain times and under certain conditions, however, various land-born insects, called terrestrials, can represent a significant segment of the trout's food supply. By midsummer, on some rivers, most of the larger mayflies and stone flies have emerged, and the quantity of nymphal life is greatly reduced. The remaining hatches are made up mainly of minute species, such as *Baetis* and *Tricorythodes,* and the immature nymphs from the earlier hatches are microscopic in size. This decreasing underwater food supply, coupled with the increasing availability of terrestrials, sets the stage for some very exciting fishing.

Many anglers retire their rods about this time of the year, feeling that the season is over. Others become discouraged at low-water conditions and high temperatures, while some claim the streams are all fished out. The truth of the matter is, trout turn at this period to various terrestrials that supplement their basic diet of small aquatic insects. Land-born insects such as grasshoppers, crickets, beetles, leafhoppers, and ants become increasingly more important as the summer progresses. These creatures are not aquatic but their availability to the trout is produced when they either jump, fall, fly, or get blown into the water. Except on rare occasions, insects such as grasshoppers, beetles, and crickets are not accessible to the fish in great numbers. However, they provide a juicy morsel for the trout at a time when his basic food supply is declining and, as a result, very few floating specimens are required to trigger frenzied feeding activity. It is amazing sometimes how far a fish will move from his normal feeding position to take some of the larger terrestrials.

On the other hand, smaller terrestrials cause gentle unhurried rises that more closely resemble the feeding activity associated with hatches of small mayflies and midges. These include ants, flying ants, leafhoppers, treehoppers, and small beetles. Of this group, the flying ants appear in greater numbers and cause more surface activity than any of the others.

Most of our study has been focused on aquatic insects, but we feel that attention should be given to some of the more important terrestrials. The following includes minimal descriptive information and one or more suggested patterns.

GRASSHOPPERS

Grasshoppers belong to the order Orthoptera and have an incomplete life cycle. The adults vary greatly in size, have relatively long antennae, and most are greenish or yellowish gray in coloration. Four wings lie flat over the body; the hind pair folds fanlike under the front pair, which are straight and exhibit a leathery texture, while the rear legs are longer than the others and are characterized by large muscular femurs. These strong levers, or kickers, provide grasshoppers with the ability to propel themselves into the air with great force. This fact makes them difficult to capture for observation purposes, but fortunately for the fly-fisherman, contributes to their presence in the stream. Once the trout have become oriented to these low-floating silhouettes and have sampled a few nourishing mouthfuls, some fantastic fishing is possible. This period can begin by mid-July and usually peaks in August, lasting for the balance of the season. During these peak periods, large trout can be found at midday lying in some very peculiar places. They just seem to be waiting for the hoppers to come floating down. Feeding lanes normally quite narrow become very wide; in fact, a fly thrown within the trout's range of detection is simply not safe! At other times, when the fish are not quite so cooperative or anxious, various techniques may be required. Generally, a dead drift is adequate, but a well-timed twitch can be extremely effective on occasion. Frequently, bouncing the artificial off a rock or a grassy bank produces the most action, while at other times the splash produced by a vigorous hard-driving cast can be the key to success. Imitations should float low in the water to properly simulate the profile and position of the natural.

Of the many patterns that have been developed to imitate grasshoppers,

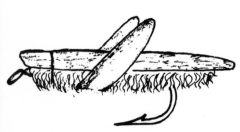

Quill-bodied hopper—the body is solid turkey quill covered with mohlon; the kickers are small turkey quills; the wings are turkey segments

most are very effective when used at the proper time. Rather than listing all of these specific patterns here, some general tying information will be offered along with a couple of favorite patterns. The outstanding features of the hopper include body, legs, and wings, in that order. Bodies are robust and can be imitated effectively with dubbing, synthetic yarns, and clipped deer hair dyed to the color desired. Legs, especially the hind pair, are quite significant in the outline and best simulated with quills, herl, and strands of pheasant-tail fibers. Hair, such as deer body hair and woodchuck, and mottled turkey make excellent wings.

Turkey Wing Hopper

BODY	yellow mohlon, extended or looped beyond bend of hook, forms a robust body all the way to the eye
WINGS	mottled turkey-quill segments laid flat over and slightly beyond body, lash down behind head area and trim butts over front of head
LEGS	several pheasant-tail fibers knotted and looped, on each side one third of the way back on body

Turkey Wing Hopper

Deer Hair Hopper

BODY	yellow deer hair spun and clipped to shape, leave room for head
WINGS	natural deer hair—or light and dark elk hair, mixed —tied over and beyond body, flared slightly, clip butts to form head

Deer Hair Hopper

CRICKETS

The cricket, another member of the order Orthoptera, also represents a food source for the trout at certain times of the season. They vary widely in shape and structure, but most are of black coloration. Like grasshoppers, the crickets have an incomplete life cycle and have chewing mouth parts. They overwinter underground in the egg stage or survive in protected areas in the nymphal stage. Crickets have four wings folded over their back that are seldom, if ever, used for flying. They also have long antennae and strong "kickers," similar to the hoppers. Finding crickets in the stream is not nearly as common as finding grasshoppers, but when present they are considered a special treat by the trout. Techniques used when fishing cricket imitations parallel quite closely those utilized for hoppers.

Deer Hair Cricket—Impressionistic

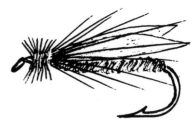

BODY	black fur
WINGS	crow-quill segments
HEAD-HACKLE	black deer hair, tips flared for hackle, butts clipped to form head

Deer Hair Cricket (impressionistic)

Deer Hair Cricket—Realistic

BODY	black deer hair, segmented underbody with overlay
TAILS	two black goose-quill segments, half of body length
HEAD	formed from clipping butts from body material
LEGS	front and middle pair out of medium black goose-quill segments, rear kickers out of heavy black goose-quill segments
ANTENNAE	two black polar bear hairs

Deer Hair Cricket (realistic)

LEAFHOPPERS AND TREEHOPPERS

These little creatures, called jassids, are members of the order Homoptera, which is closely related to the order Hemiptera, or true bugs. They display great variation in size and color and are equipped with mouth parts that can be used for piercing and sucking. Winged species have two pairs of wings, with the front pair longer and narrower than the hind pair. The wings are folded rooflike over the back and are opaque and leathery in appearance. Jassids feed on a wide variety of plant life and can be present in great numbers. Nymphs are difficult to locate because they are very active. When a plant on which they are feeding is disturbed, they scurry to the opposite side of the leaf. The nymphs also have the strange habit of moving sideways rather than forward. Being small and light, the adults are easily blown into the stream where they provide food for the trout and a challenge to the fisherman. Imitations must be tied on small hooks, usually size #22 to #28, but are simple to construct.

JASSID

BODY	tying thread matched to body color of natural
HACKLE	small dry-fly quality, palmered, matched to natural, brown, black, ginger, and grizzly are all good, trimmed top and bottom
WINGS	two jungle-cock nails or quail-breast feathers tied flat over body

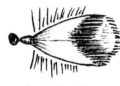

Quail Jassid

BEETLES

One of the largest orders of insects are the Coleoptera, or "sheath wings." This group of insects have complete life cycles, chewing mouth parts, and four wings. The front wings are leathery and fit over the hind part of the body like a case, meeting in a straight line along the center of the back. The hind wings are clear, and fold under the front wings when the insect is at rest. Real beetles, such as ladybird beetles, potato beetles, and click beetles, are quite important as a trout food, mainly because of their abundance. Rotted logs, overhanging foliage, wooded areas, and grassy banks all provide a possible habitat for beetles. Many are deposited in the stream by high water or are blown in by the wind. Even when they are present on the water in large numbers, it can be difficult for the occasional fisherman to detect them. Their low-water profile is not easy to perceive unless a close study of the water is made. The increased activity of Japanese beetles has resulted in some excellent fishing in the affected areas. Patterns with opaque flat shapes and low-floating qualities are necessary for proper simulation.

JAPANESE BEETLE

BODY   green tying thread
HACKLE   brown and grizzly palmered and trimmed top and bottom
WINGS   three or four iridescent green neck feathers from a cock pheasant laid atop each other and lacquered

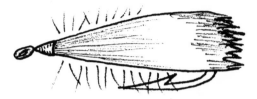

Japanese Beetle

BLACK BEETLE

BODY   peacock herl
HACKLE   black, palmered
WINGS   black quill segment laid over whole body

Black Beetle

ANTS

Ants belong to the order Hymenoptera, or "membrane wings," and have a complete life cycle. They vary considerably in size and have three distinct body regions. The four clear wings, when present, have simple venation, with the hind pair smaller than the front wings. Actually, ants are wingless except at swarming time, when they suddenly become of great interest to the angler. Some of the finest feeding activity of the season takes place when the swarming flights occur. In order to take advantage of the situation one must stay alert and be prepared to swing into action quickly.

Several things can happen when the ants begin to swarm, all of which could cause problems for the angler. First, if the ants float along with their wings in an upright position they can be mistaken for mayflies and, unfortunately, mayfly patterns do not work very well when ants are on the water. Even if the mayfly imitation is of the proper size and coloration, it is not effective because the shape of an ant body is vastly different from that of a mayfly. However, on the water this fact is difficult for the angler to perceive; he can see only upright wings, which normally would suggest that mayflies are on the water. Many times we've wasted a good share of the flying-ant "hatch" by flailing the water with a mayfly pattern.

If the ants have their wings in a spent position, then the problem is visibility. It's almost impossible to see spent-wing ants riding in the film. Their clear membrane wings and minute low-floating bodies can only be detected by close observation. This, of course, can quickly be solved by utilizing the fine-mesh hand net to capture a sample. One other problem is

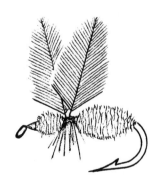

Hen-wing ant with "V" hackle

that the swarm often descends very quickly, causing extraordinary, but short-lived, feeding activity. When this happens the angler must react immediately in order to take advantage of the situation.

Wingless ant imitations are very effective throughout the warmer months of the season. They are fished wet or dry and can provide real excitement during some of the so-called dead periods of the day. Fishing the wingless pattern calls for a technique differing from the one utilized for the winged variety. The fall of a swarm of flying ants results in casting for rising trout which closely parallels the technique used when aquatic insects are emerging. However, wingless ants are not normally on the water in such great multitudes as to cause either a general rise or extensive feeding activity. As a result, the creative angler must change his approach and cast to areas where ants might be falling into the water. These areas may be located under overhanging boughs near grassy shorelines, or around fallen logs. Fine leaders, a cautious approach, and delicate casting contribute immensely to the effectiveness of the technique.

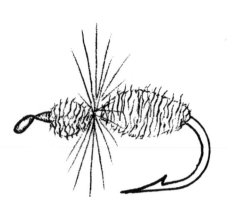

Ant (wet or dry)

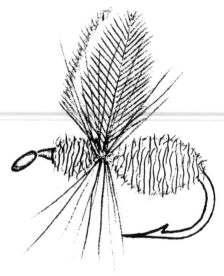

Hen-wing ant
(conventional hackle)

BLACK ANT

BODY   black dubbing, form two lumps, larger one at the rear of shank and smaller one behind the eye, separated by a thin waist

HACKLE   high-quality natural black, very sparse, tied in right behind front lump

CINNAMON-AND-BROWN FLYING ANT—SPENT

BODY   large lump at rear of shank out of dark- to medium-brown dubbing, front lump and thin waist out of cinnamon dubbing, use dark brown tying thread to form head

WINGS AND HACKLE   bronze blue dun tied in immediately behind front lump and trimmed top and bottom

LARGE CINNAMON FLYING ANT—UPRIGHT WINGS

BODY   rear lump and front lump out of cinnamon dubbing, use cinnamon tying thread to form head

WING   light-gray hackle tips or shaped light-gray feather tied in immediately behind front lump in upright position, slightly spread

HACKLE   bronze blue dun, sparse and trimmed on bottom

The Black Ant dressing is a general pattern that can be tied in size #14 to #28 and can be fished wet or dry. In the smaller sizes, #20 to #28, great care should be taken to keep the hackle small and sparse in order to maintain proper body silhouette. The small cinnamon-and-brown ant and the larger cinnamon ant are both specific flies that appear on Michigan's Au Sable River in late August and early September. A size #22 hook should be used for the cinnamon-and-brown pattern while the larger all-cinnamon species is best imitated on a size #18. Each type should be tied with upright and spent wings. On the Au Sable, both of these ants are on the water at the same time, producing a difficult situation in itself. Things get further complicated, however, due to the fact that at least one, and sometimes two, of the better mayfly hatches of the season are also occurring. On top of all this, the ants often are sporadic—that is, they will fall two or three times in one evening rather than all at once. These combined factors can produce a feeding situation that is constantly changing and the angler must, therefore, remain alert and extremely observant. When these conditions develop, the fish normally feed on the insects most numerous on the water. The effective fly-fisherman must be able to detect any variation in feeding conditions and then quickly make the proper correction in pattern and presentation.

GREEN WORM

Green oak worms build their nests in trees and groups of them can be found in tentlike structures. During a two-week period, usually in June, they come out and hang down by a silk thread, sometimes dangling over and falling in the water. In locations where this phenomenon takes place, trout, often large trout, are on the lookout for them. They make a juicy morsel and autopsies performed by local guides show stomachs of trout to be crammed full during the season.

IMITATION GREEN WORM

BODY   greenish-yellowish deer body hair clipped, hook size #8 to #12

Deer Hair Green Worm, spun and shaped

CHAPTER 12

The "Super Hatches"

IN AN ATTEMPT to keep the number of patterns to a minimum, we have devised the concept of "Super Hatches" for each section of the country. Probably 80 percent of all fly-fishing to rising trout during a season would be to these insects. So it is logical that we should concentrate on these hatches. From our experience, we feel there are only eight mayflies of major significance in each area. In many cases, imitation of only one or two stages is necessary to fish a certain hatch properly, thus reducing the number of artificials to be carried in our already overloaded fishing vests. The following charts list the Super Hatches of the East, Midwest, and West along with peak emergence periods and patterns required for imitating the important stages of each species.

Listed patterns and corresponding dressings can be found in the Master List of Patterns, immediately following the charts. From this Master List, an angler from any section of the country can, at a glance, determine which patterns he must carry and what size they should be. Flytiers can also tie from this list.

It can be seen from the Master List of Patterns that only eight artificials

Hendrickson nymph (*Ephemerella subvaria*)

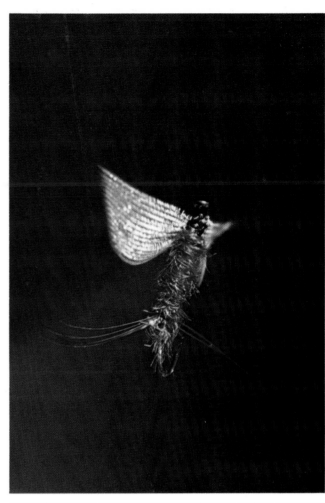

Hendrickson nymph, #14

Hendrickson No-Hackle Dun, #14 (*from underwater*)

Hendrickson (*Ephemerella subvaria*, male dun)

Hendrickson Spinner, #14 (top view)

Wiggle Nymph, #18 (for Pale Morning Dun)

Hendrickson (*Ephemerella subvaria*, male spinner)

Pale Morning Dun nymph (*Ephemerella infrequens*)

Gray-wing Olive Paradun, #16 *(from underwater)*

Half-spent Olive Hen Spinner, #16

Pale Morning Dun *(Ephemerella infrequens,* female)

Pale Morning Dun *(Ephemerella infrequens,* spinner)

Western Slate-wing Olive Dun (*Ephemerella flavilinea*, female dun)

Gray Drake (Western) (*Siphlonurus occidentalis*, female dun)

Speckled Dun (*Callibaetis coloradensis*, male dun)

Small Blue-wing Olive (*Baetis hiemalis*, from underwater)

Female Brown Drake Dun (*Ephemera simulans*)

Giant Michigan Mayfly (*Hexagenia limbata*)

Light Cahill (*Stenonema canadenses*, female dun)

Pale Evening Dun (*Ephemerella dorothea*, female dun)

Pale Morning Dun (*Ephemerella lacustris*, male dun)

Tiny White-wing Black Spinner (*Tricorithodes stigiatus*)

Grey Fox (*Stenonema fuscum*, female dun)

Tiny Gray-wing Olive (*Pseudocloeon anoka*, female dun)

Green Drake Spinner (*Ephemera guttulata*, female, Eastern)

Western Slate-wing Olive (*Ephemerella flavilinea*, spinner)

Speckled Spinner (*Callibaetis nigritus*, female spinner)

Pale Morning Dun (*Ephemerella dorothea*, female spinner)

Green Drake nymph (*Ephemera guttalata*, Eastern)

Green Caddis pupa

Brown Drake nymph (*Ephemera simulans*)

Brown Midge pupa

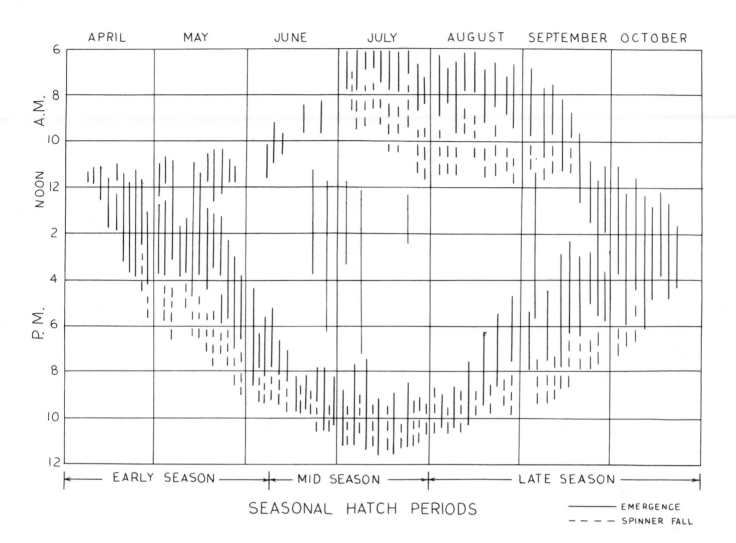

SEASONAL HATCH PERIODS

———— EMERGENCE
– – – – SPINNER FALL

are required for the Eastern Super Hatches, nine for the Midwest and nine for the West. For the entire country, only eleven mayfly patterns are needed to fish all the species.

The Master Patterns will not only imitate the Super Hatches effectively but they can also be used for many other hatches. The following list includes the Master Patterns and the species they simulate.

An additional list containing the minimum number of patterns to fish caddis flies, stone flies and midges effectively is presented below.

EASTERN SUPER HATCHES

Genus and Species (Common Name) Size	PEAK EMERGENCE							STAGE			PATTERNS REQUIRED	
	April	May	June	July	Aug.	Sept.	Oct.	N	D	S	No.	Name
Epeorus pleuralis (Gordon Quill) #14 or #16	20——10							X	X		1 2	Slate/Brown Emerger Slate/Tan No-Hackle
Ephemerella subvaria (Hendrickson) #12 or #14	25——20							X	X	X	1 2 11	Slate/Brown Emerger Slate/Tan Paradun Dun/Brown Hen Spinner
Ephemerella dorothea (Sulphur Dun) #16 or #18		20———————5							X	X	9 11	Gray/Yellow No-Hackle Dun/Brown Hen Spinner
Stenonema fuscum (Gray Fox) #10 or #12		25——15							X		2	Slate/Tan Paradun
Ephemera guttulata (Green Drake) #8 or #10			1—10						X	X	9 13	Gray/Yellow Paradun Dun/Cream Hen Spinner
Ephemerella attenuata (Slate-wing Olive Dun) #16 or #18			10——1						X		8	Slate/Olive No-Hackle
Tricorythodes species (Tiny White-wing Black) #24 to #28				5———————10						X	14	White/Black Hen Spinner
Baetis species (Blue-wing Olive) #18 to #24	25						15		X		7	Gray/Olive No-Hackle

MIDWESTERN SUPER HATCHES

Genus and Species (Common Name) Size	PEAK EMERGENCE							STAGE			PATTERNS REQUIRED	
	April	May	June	July	Aug.	Sept.	Oct.	N	D	S	No.	Name
Ephemerella subvaria (Hendrickson) #12 or #14	25——	25						X	X	X	1 2 11	Slate/Brown Emerger Slate/Tan Paradun Dun/Brown Hen Spinner
Ephemerella dorothea (Sulphur Dun) #16 or #18		25——		——5					X	X	9 11	Gray/Yellow No-Hackle Dun/Brown Hen Spinner
Ephemera simulans (Brown Drake) #10 or #12			1—20						X	X	9 12	Gray/Yellow Paradun Dun/Yellow Hen Spinner
Pseudocloeon anoka (Tiny Blue-wing Olive) #24			20——	——20		1—30			X	X	6 11	Dun/Olive No-Hackle Dun/Brown Hen Spinner
Hexagenia limbata (Giant Michigan Mayfly) #4 to #8			25——	——20					X	X	9 12	Gray/Yellow No-Hackle Dun/Yellow Hen Spinner
Ephemerella lata (Slate-wing Olive Dun) #18 to #20				5——	——5				X	X	8 11	Slate/Olive Paradun Dun/Brown Hen Spinner
Tricorythodes species (Tiny White-wing Black) #24 to #28				10——		——15				X	14	White/Black Hen Spinner
Baetis species (Blue-wing Olive) #16 to #24	25——						15		X		7	Gray/Olive No-Hackle

WESTERN SUPER HATCHES

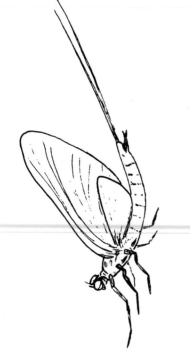

Genus and Species (Common Name) Size	PEAK EMERGENCE							STAGE			PATTERNS REQUIRED	
	April	May	June	July	Aug.	Sept.	Oct.	N	D	S	No.	Name
Epeorus and Paraleptophlebia species (Slate-wing Drakes) #12 to #16			1				5		X		5	Slate/Brown Paradun
Ephemerella inermis group (Pale Morning Duns) #16 to #22			5				30	X	X	X	1 9 11	Slate/Brown Emerger Gray/Yellow No-Hackle Dun/Brown Hen Spinner
Heptagenia and Siphlonurus species (Western Gray Drakes) #10 to #18			10			25			X		2	Slate/Tan Paradun
Ephemerella grandis (Western Green Drake) #8 or #10			15	15				X	X		1 8	Slate/Brown Emerger Slate/Olive Paradun
Callibaetis species (Speckled Spinner) #14 or #16			20			30			X	X	2 13	Slate/Tan No-Hackle Dun/Cream Hen Spinner
Ephemerella flavilinea (Slate-wing Olive Dun) #14 or #16			25		15			X	X	X	1 8 11	Slate/Brown Emerger Slate/Olive No-Hackle Dun/Brown Hen Spinner
Tricorythodes species (Tiny White-wing Black) #22 to #28				20		30				X	14	White/Black Hen Spinner
Baetis species (Blue-wing Olive) #18 to #24		1					30		X		7	Gray/Olive No-Hackle

MASTER LIST OF PATTERNS

No.	Wing/Body Type	Wings*	Body†	Tails	Hackle‡	East	Midwest	West
1	Slate/Brown Emerger	dark gray hackle tips	brown fur	partridge or wood duck	partridge or wood duck	#12 to #16	#12 or #14	#8 or #10 #14 to #22
2	Slate/Tan Paradun	dark gray hen-hackle fibers	tan fur	gray hackle fibers	dark gray	#10 to #16	#12 or #14	#10 to #18
	Slate/Tan No-Hackle	dark gray duck shoulder	tan fur	gray hackle fibers	none			
3	Dun/Brown Paradun	light gray hen-hackle fibers	brown fur	gray hackle fibers	light gray			
	Dun/Brown No-Hackle	light gray duck shoulder	brown fur	gray hackle fibers	none			
4	Gray/Brown Paradun	gray hen-hackle fibers	brown fur	gray hackle fibers	gray			
	Gray/Brown No-Hackle	gray duck shoulder	brown fur	gray hackle fibers	none			#12 to #16
5	Slate/Brown Paradun	dark gray hen-hackle fibers	brown fur	gray hackle fibers	dark gray			
	Slate/Brown No-Hackle	dark gray duck shoulder	brown fur	gray hackle fibers	none			
6	Dun/Olive Paradun	light gray hen-hackle fibers	olive fur	gray hackle fibers	light gray		#24	
	Dun/Olive No-Hackle	light gray duck shoulder	olive fur	gray hackle fibers	none			
7	Gray/Olive Paradun	gray hen-hackle fibers	olive fur	gray hackle fibers	gray	#16 to #24	#18 to #24	#18 to #24
	Gray/Olive No-Hackle	gray duck shoulder	olive fur	gray hackle fibers	none			
8	Slate/Olive Paradun	dark gray hen-hackle fibers	olive fur	gray hackle fibers	dark gray	#16 to #18	#18 or #20	#8 or #10
	Slate/Olive No-Hackle	dark gray duck shoulder	olive fur	gray hackle fibers	none			#14 or #16

* For Paraduns size #12 and larger, use hair (such as elk or deer) for clump wings, replacing hackle fibers.
† Use Rabbit for all furs, except as otherwise noted.
‡ For no-hackles, wings can also be paired duck-quill segments, partridge, or turkey breast.

MASTER LIST OF PATTERNS (continued)

No.	Wing/Body Type	Wings*	Body†	Tails	Hackle‡	East	Midwest	West
9	Gray/Yellow Paradun	gray hen-hackle fibers	yellow fur	gray hackle fibers	gray	#8 to #10 &	#4 to #12 &	#16 to #22
	Gray/Yellow No-Hackle	gray duck shoulder	yellow fur	gray hackle fibers	none	#16 to #18	#16 or #18	
10	Cream/Yellow Paradun	cream hen-hackle fibers	yellow fur	gray hackle fibers	cream			
	Cream/Yellow No-Hackle	cream duck shoulder	yellow fur	gray hackle fibers	none			
11	Dun/Brown Hen Spinner	light gray hen tips	brown fur	gray hackle fibers	none	#12 to #18	#12 to #20	#14 to #22
	Dun/Brown Partridge Spinner	gray partridge	brown fur	gray hackle fibers	none			
	Dun/Brown Hackle Spinner	light gray hackle	brown fur	gray hackle fibers	gray, sometimes clipped top and bottom			
12	Dun/Yellow Hen Spinner	light gray hen tips	yellow fur	gray hackle fibers	sparse gray or none		#4 to #12	
	Dun/Yellow Partridge Spinner	gray partridge	yellow fur	gray hackle fibers	sparse gray or none			
	Dun/Yellow Hackle Spinner	light gray hackle	yellow fur	gray hackle fibers	gray, sometimes clipped top and bottom			
13	Dun/Cream Hen Spinner	light gray hen tips	German fitch	gray hackle fibers	sparse gray or none	#8 to #10		#14 or #16
	Dun/Cream Partridge Spinner	gray partridge	cream fur	gray hackle fibers	sparse gray or none			
	Dun/Cream Hackle Spinner	light gray hackle		gray hackle fibers	gray, sometimes clipped top and bottom			
14	White/Black Hen Spinner	light gray hen tips	dark mole fur	gray hackle fibers	none	#24 to #28	#24 to #28	#22 to #28
	White/Black Partridge Spinner	gray partridge	dark mole fur	gray hackle fibers	none			
	White/Black Hackle Spinner	light gray hackle	dark mole fur	gray hackle fibers	gray, sometimes clipped top and bottom			

* For Paraduns size #12 and larger, use hair (such as elk or deer) for clump wings, replacing hackle fibers.
† Use Rabbit for all furs, except as otherwise noted.
‡ For no-hackles, wings can also be paired duck-quill segments, partridge, or turkey breast.

NYMPHS

1   SLATE/BROWN EMERGER—EFFECTIVE FOR THE MAJORITY OF SPECIES

DUNS

2   SLATE/TAN PARADUN OR NO-HACKLE

Genus:	*Ephemerella*	**Species:**	*subvaria*
			invaria
			rotunda
	Epeorus		*pleuralis*
			longimanus
	Siphlonurus		*rapidus*
			quebecensis
			columbianus
			occidentalis
	Stenonema		*ithaca*
			fuscum
			vicarium
	Heptagenia		*elegantula*
	Callibaetis		*nigritus*
			coloradensis

3   DUN/BROWN PARADUN OR NO-HACKLE

Genus:	*Baetis*	**Species:**	*tricaudatus*
			bicaudatus
			alexanderi

4   GRAY/BROWN PARADUN OR NO-HACKLE

Genus:	*Baetis*	**Species:**	*cingulatus*
			phoebus
	Callibaetis		*americanus*
	Heptagenia		*criddlei*

5   SLATE/BROWN PARADUN OR NO-HACKLE

Genus:	*Baetis*	**Species:**	*vagans*
			hiemalis
			parvus
	Callibaetis		*fluctuans*
	Isonychia		*bicolor*
	Epeorus		*nitidus*
			grandis

Cinygmula	*ramaleyi*
Rhithrogena	*jejuna*
Leptophlebia	*johnsoni*
	cupida
Paraleptophlebia	*adoptiva*
	debilis

6 DUN/OLIVE PARADUN OR NO-HACKLE

Genus: *Ephemerella*   **Species:** *extrucians*

Pseudocloeon   *anoka*
                       edmundsi

Cloeon   *implicatum*

7 GRAY/OLIVE PARADUN OR NO-HACKLE

Genus: *Baetis*   **Species:** *levitans*
                                  pygmaeus

8 SLATE/OLIVE PARADUN OR NO-HACKLE

Genus: *Ephemerella*   **Species:** *lata*
                                  attenuata
                                  walkeri
                                  needhami
                                  grandis
                                  flavilinea

Paraleptophlebia   *packi*

9 GRAY/YELLOW PARADUN OR NO-HACKLE

Genus: *Ephemerella*   **Species:** *dorothea*
                                  inermis
                                  infrequens
                                  lacustris

Epeorus   *vitrea*
                        deceptivus

Heptagenia   *simplicioides*

10 CREAM/YELLOW PARADUN OR NO-HACKLE

Genus: *Stenonema*   **Species:** *canadense*
                                  frontale
                                  interpunctatum
                                  heterotarsale

Potamanthus   *distinctus*

SPINNERS

11 DUN/BROWN HEN SPINNER, PARTRIDGE SPINNER OR HACKLE SPINNER

Genus:	*Ephemerella*	**Species:**	all
	Baetis		all
	Callibaetis		all
	Isonychia		all
	Siphlonurus		all
	Heptagenia		*criddlei*
			elegantula
	Epeorus		*longimanus*
			nitidus
			grandis
			deceptivus
	Cinygmula		*ramaleyi*
	Rhithrogena		*jejuna*
	Leptophlebia		all
	Paraleptophlebia		all

12 DUN/YELLOW HEN SPINNER, PARTRIDGE SPINNER, OR HACKLE SPINNER

Genus:	*Ephemera*	**Species:**	*simulans*
	Hexagenia		*limbata*
	Potamanthus		*distinctus*

13 DUN/CREAM HEN SPINNER, PARTRIDGE SPINNER OR HACKLE SPINNER

Genus:	*Stenonema*	**Species:**	*canadense* group
	Ephemera		*guttulata*
			varia
	Heptagenia		*simplicioides*
	Epeorus		*pleuralis*
			vitrea
			albertae
	Callibaetis		*coloradensis*
			nigritus

14 WHITE/BLACK HEN SPINNER, PARTRIDGE SPINNER, OR HACKLE SPINNER

Genus:	*Tricorythodes*	**Species:**	*stygiatus*
			atratus
			minutus
	Brachycercus		*lacustris*
			prudens

CADDIS FLY PATTERNS

(1) Groundhog/Tan #14 to #22   (4) Tan Pupa #14 to #22
(2) Groundhog/Green #14 to #22   (5) Green Pupa #14 to #22
(3) Groundhog/Gray # 14 to #22   (6) Gray Pupa #14 to #22

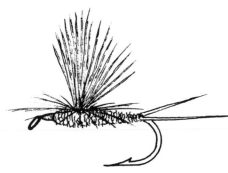

Natural hen-hackle fiber
paradun

STONE FLY PATTERNS

(1) Groundhog/Yellow # 12 to #20
(2) Groundhog/Tannish Olive #12 to #20

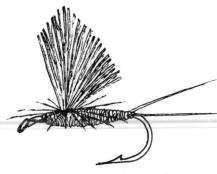

Shaped hen-hackle fiber
paradun

MIDGE PATTERNS

(1) Gray Midge #22 to #28   (2) Olive Pupa #22 to #28

By adding these ten imitations to his eleven basic mayfly patterns, an angler can cover almost any hatch in any section of the country. *At least 90 percent of our fishing time is spent utilizing these flies.*

Most of these imitations lack popular names, so we have given the types we use the most general designations, such as Paradun, No-Hackle, Hen Spinner, Partridge Spinner and Hackle Spinner. Two colors appear in front of these titles, the first indicating the shade of the wing and the second giving the general coloration of the body. In our system of classifying wing color, slate is dark gray, gray is medium gray, and dun is light gray. Bodies are much more difficult to group, due to the multitude of colors found in many species. The body color used in our pattern names is the one that we feel is predominant, even though others may be present. For instance, the body colors in the spinners of *E. inermis* during the same fall vary from dark brown to olive tan, so a general match-up is usually effective.

PARADUN TYPE

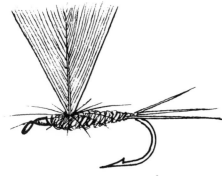

Turkey clump paradun

These artificials usually have clump wings encircled with parachute hackle and are used to simulate freshly hatched duns, hence the name paradun. For smaller flies, wing clumps are normally comprised of webby fibers from a hen-hackle feather, but for larger flies, either deer body hair, elk hair, or impala is more desirable. The parachute hackle is kept short, only ⅔ as long as the wings, and very sparse, two or three turns, so it does not obliterate the wing outline. It is normally the same general coloration as the wings.

Tails are constructed of stiff hackle fibers and spread widely for balance. Bodies are made of various kinds of fur such as mole, rabbit, and muskrat, either natural or dyed to the proper color. They are spun on the tying thread by taking a small amount and spinning it with the thumb and forefinger and then wound conventionally until the desired size and shape is achieved. For some hatches, a more realistic appearance is obtained by blending two or more colors. These furs are best for size #10 and smaller. For large flies, an extended deer- or elk-hair body is very effective.

HOW TO TIE AN EXTENDED-BODY DRY FLY

1. Have hook in vice with tails tied in and tying thread at front of hook

2. Take a bunch of hollow hair, such as deer or elk hair, and lay parallel to and surrounding hook shank

3. Take tying thread and wrap around hair, just as you would ribbing, to the length you desire the body to be

4. Take a few turns around the end or tip of body and reverse direction of thread, tying back toward head of hook to give crisscross ribbing effect on the body

5. Tie in a clump of elk hair or other wing material

6. Wind short stiff hackle three or four times around base of wing clump, and finish off

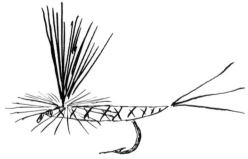

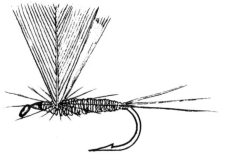

Turkey paradun

Hair wings

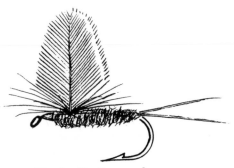

Hen-hackle tip paradun

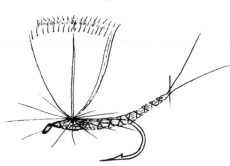

Shoulder feather wings

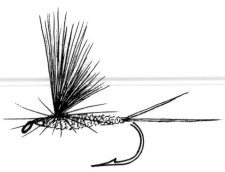

Natural hen-hackle fiber paradun—set on an angle to simulate true shape

Elk hair wings

B = body length
W = wing length = B
W₁ = wing width = 30% of B
T = tail length = B

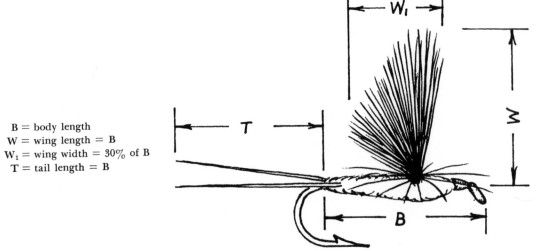

HOW TO TIE THE PARADUN PATTERNS

1. Spin tuft of fur on tying thread

2. Wrap tuft of fur on rear of shank

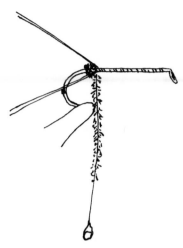

3. Tie in wisps of cock hackles on both sides of fur tuft so tails are widely spread and then spin more fur on tying thread for body

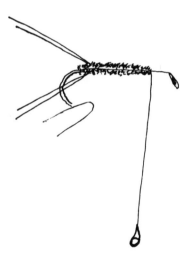

4. Wrap fur to head of hook to form body

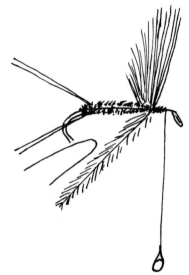

5. Tie a clump of hen-hackle fibers and clip to shape of a mayfly wing. On large flies use elk hair for wing clump. Tie a small cock hackle feather close to clump wing.

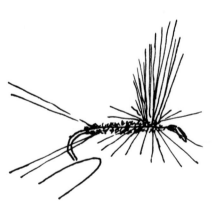

6. Wind hackle feather around base of clump two or three turns and finish off

NO-HACKLE TYPE

Wings are usually made from small duck-shoulder feathers that are readily available in many shades of gray. They look like a small fan-wing, but present a more mayflylike silhouette, slimming down when wet. Other effective wings for no-hackle flies can be constructed with a clump of hen-hackle fibers. These are very durable and look realistic on the water and are suitable for smaller flies. Duck-quill segments also make excellent wings. Tails are generally the color of the wings and are widely split for positioning of the fly. Bodies are made of fur, which when well dressed floats the artificial

Duck-quill segment no-hackle

TYING THE NO-HACKLE DRY FLY

1. Spin tuft of fur on tying thread

2. Wrap tuft of fur on rear of shank

3. Tie in wisps of cock hackles on both sides of fur tuft, so tails are widely spread and then spin more fur on tying thread for body

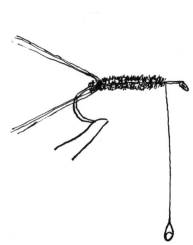

4. Wrap fur to head of hook to form body

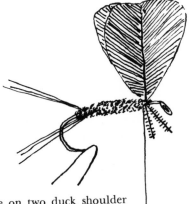

5. Tie on two duck shoulder feathers with clipped stems. Do not strip stems as this weakens them considerably. Duck pointer quills can also be used.

6. Wind in a little more spun fur in front of wings to form a thorax, and then finish off

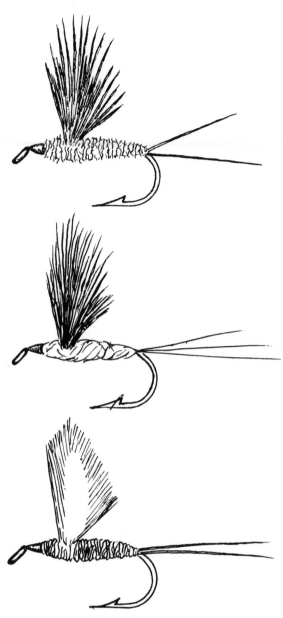

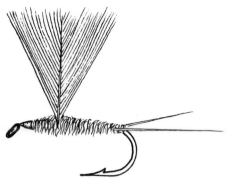

Turkey clump no-hackle

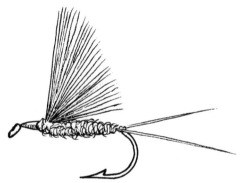

Paired turkey no-hackle

Three no-hackle types using
natural hen-hackle fiber

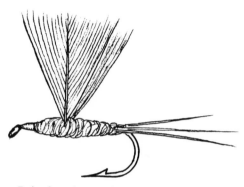

Turkey fiber no-hackle (set on
an angle)

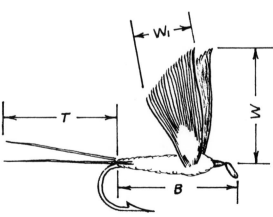

B = body length
W = wing length = B
W₁ = wing width = 30% of B
T = tail length = B

Shaped hen hackle fiber no hackle

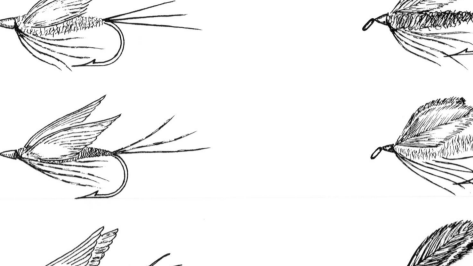

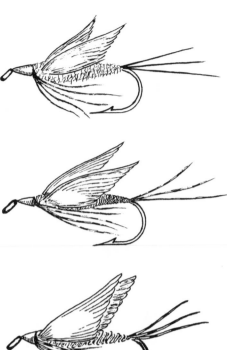

Three duck-quill segment emergers

Three hackle-tip emergers

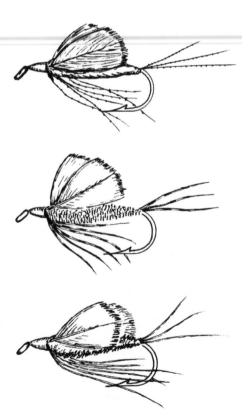

Turkey clump emerger

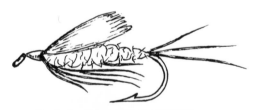

Duck-shoulder clump emerger

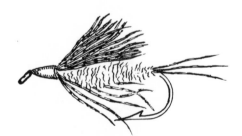

Three duck-shoulder emergers

Partridge emerger

just as well as a fully hackled version. Without hackle, the wing outline is pure and the distorting effect is eliminated.

EMERGER TYPE

Bodies are made of fur and the emergent wings are hackle tips slanted back and extending ¾ the length of the body. Tails and legs are best imitated with partridge or wood duck. These artificials can be fished wet or dry depending on the weight of the hook and whether or not dressing is applied.

HEN SPINNER TYPE

These flies are tied with hen-hackle-tip wings in the full spent position. Hen hackle is broader and more webby than rooster hackle, and lying awash in the film, it becomes translucent and presents a supremely realistic outline. If well dressed, these wings absorb the dressing, not water, so they actually help float the fly. Bodies on the smaller flies are made of fur and hackle is not required. On larger flies, an extended hair body is very effective.

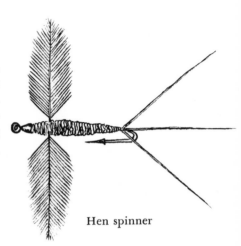

Hen spinner

HOW TO TIE THE EMERGER PATTERNS

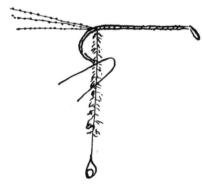

1. Tie in three tail fibers (cock hackle wisps, wood-duck fibers, or partridge breast fibers) and spin fur on tying thread

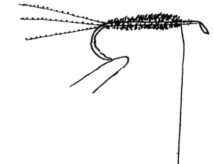

2. Wind on tying thread with fur up to head of hook to form body

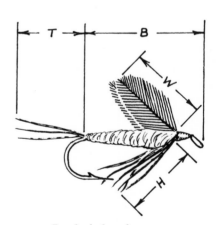

B = body length
W = wing length = ¾B
H = hackle length = ¾B
T = tail length = ½ to ¾B

3. Tie in wisps of partridge, wood-duck, or hackle fibers, for legs

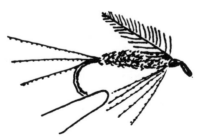

4. Tie in two short hackle tips, slanting back over body to form emerging wings, and then finish off

1. Spin tuft of fur on tying thread

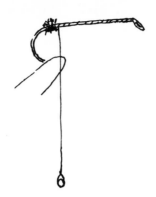

2. Wrap tuft of fur on rear of shank

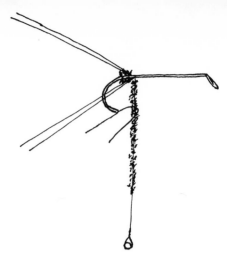

3. Tie in wisps of cock hackles on both sides of fur tuft so tails are widely spread and then spin more fur on tying thread for **body**

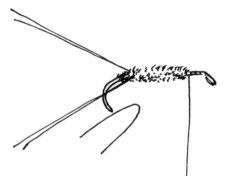

4. Wrap fur to head of hook to form **body**

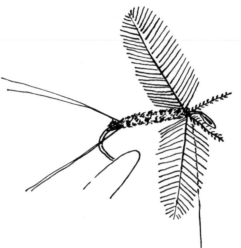

5. Tie in two hen hackle tips (either half-spent or full spent, as desired). Do not strip the butts of the hackle feathers as this weakens them; clip butts with scissors.

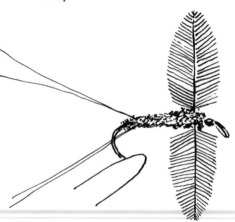

6. Spin more thread on tying silk and wrap around wing to form thorax, and then finish. Tails on spinners should be much longer than on dun imitations.

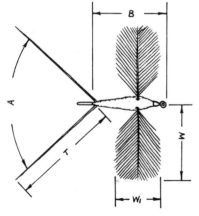

B = body length
W = wing length = B
W₁ = wing width = 30% of B
T = tail length = 1½B
A = tail-split angle = 45°

PARTRIDGE SPINNER TYPE

This is also a no-hackle type of pattern and is similar to the hen spinner, except the wings are made of light partridge and tied either half or full spent. The fibers take on a translucent, speckled appearance when wet, resembling the hyaline wings of most spinners.

HACKLE SPINNER TYPE

Wings for these spinners are constructed of one or more hackles which are wound on in the conventional style and trimmed top and bottom. The remaining fibers protruding out the sides represent hyaline wings. They can also be trimmed half spent or left full, if a high-floating imitation of the start of the spinner fall is desired. Another version that is often very deadly is to trim just on the bottom. The same effect can be realized by criss-crossing the body material over and under the hackle so all the fibers protrude out the sides.

PARTRIDGE DRAKE

These are used to represent the larger duns. The wing is light partridge-breast feathers, usually dyed dark gray and tied on as fan wings. Bodies can be of spun fur or extended elk or deer hair. They can be no-hackle types or parachute or V hackle.

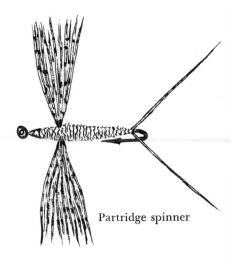

Partridge spinner

V HACKLE

Any of the dun patterns can be changed to V hackle by winding a short cock hackle in the normal manner and clipping all fibers top and bottom so that only the fibers on the side remain. These act as outriggers and this pattern lands upright amazingly well. It is the same principle as a paradun, but easier to tie.

GROUNDHOG TYPE

These flies are tied to represent caddis flies and stone flies. Groundhog hair tips are a variegated cream, tan, brown and gray which, when tied downwing style, are an excellent imitation of the folded wings of the naturals. Here again, the second part of the name indicates the color of the body. Tails are not needed and hackle is either conventional or palmered, clipped top and bottom. Bodies are rather fat as in the natural insects. These downwings can also be imitated by other feathers, such as partridge breast, mallard flank, or sections of duck primaries, or hen-hackle tips as in the hen caddis.

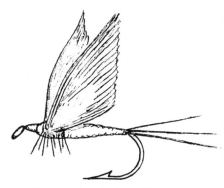

"V" hackle—duck quill segment

CADDIS PUPA TYPE

These can be tied two different ways and fished either wet or in the film. One pattern has a tapering, fat fur body with one or two turns of brown partridge. It is killing in tan, green, or gray. The other tie is the same fat body with brown partridge fibers underneath and small feather tips tied along the side as illustrated.

No-hackle caddis pupa (wet or dry)

MIDGE ADULT TYPE

These patterns imitate the natural as it hovers over the surface. Gray fur bodies with dun and grizzly hackle and dun tails are very deadly. Stiff, high-quality hackle must be used. Adults at rest, drifting on the film, are best imitated by hackle tips tied flat and divided.

MIDGE PUPA TYPE

Drifting pupas usually float in the surface film for relatively long periods of time, making imitations of this stage extremely important. These artificials are merely a thin body of fur with a thicker thorax of dark fur. Olive bodies with blackish wing pads are most common.

CHAPTER 13

Night Fishing

NIGHT IS WHEN one may expect to catch larger trout, especially browns, on flies. Large fish are unwilling to leave their hiding places during the day for fear of their arch enemies, fish-eating birds and mammals; but after dark they can roam the shallows in search of food with little or no threat of danger from most of these predators. A river that seems dead in the heat of the day often becomes alive at night, with both large and small fish ranging all over the stream in search of food.

Fishing a river in daylight and fishing the same stretch at night are extraordinarily different experiences. A wide, smooth, quiet stretch of river becomes larger, faster, deeper, and more frightening at night. But a dead river in bright daylight can become amazingly active during the witching hours. The unexpected explosion of a huge brown out of the eerie darkness is a spine-chilling experience.

Huge trout that would not dream of venturing forth in the sun can be found in the most unlikely places after dark, and often are willing to strike at the most outlandish creations of the flytier's nightmares. Baby muskrats and ducklings have been found in the autopsies of brown trout, and flies

Hair mouse

that could make a daytime dry-fly purist cringe are not only effective but enthusiastically received by nighttime advocates.

There are four main types of night fishing. The first, fishing to a spinner fall, usually occurs from dusk to an hour after dark. The second, fishing to a hatch of emerging duns, can come sporadically off and on all night long. The third type of night fishing is surface fishing to trout that are not feeding actively on a specific insect; this would include insects that are found in the water by accident—large beetles, night moths, spiders, and crane flies. The fourth type is wet-fly and streamer fishing either just below the surface or deep in the holes and runs with a sinking line.

Muddler Minnow

Dry-fly fishing to a fall of spinners begins just before dusk and since the fish can be extremely selective in these situations the need for a good pattern is imperative. Size and outline of the patterns are a little more important after dark than color, but do not ignore shades of color completely. Sometimes even a slight discrepancy in size or shape will make a pattern almost useless during these spinner falls, because returning spinners fall en masse or in a much more concentrated group than duns hatch or emerge. An emergence of duns takes place over two to three hours, whereas the spinner fall is condensed into thirty to forty-five minutes. There are far more flies on the water at a given time and these great numbers of flies falling into the water excite the trout and they often feed voraciously during these times.

Hair-wing Night Moth, hair body

It is frequently difficult after dusk to tell exactly where your artificial is among groups of naturals. Often when you think a fish is striking your artificial, he is taking a natural. And other times when a fish is actually taking your fly you might think your fly is a bit off the line and not strike. One of the ways to offset this disadvantage is to get close to the rising trout. This is possible at dusk because the fish do not seem to be bothered by the closeness of the angler if he wades in quietly.

Night moth—hair wings, Mohlon body, palmer hackle

One of our favorite patterns for the dusk spinner-fall fishing is the No-Hackle spinner. Spinner falls can range from very small insects, as small as #24 Pseudocloeons, up to an extremely large *Hexagenia limbata* or Giant Michigan mayfly. Of course, the larger the insect, the larger the trout that can be expected to feed on the fall, but even the smaller flies at dusk often entice larger fish. At this time fish usually adopt lines of drift where large numbers of insects are carried to them. They do not move far off these lines to feed, so your casting must be accurate. Hence the need to wade as close as possible so your casts may be kept short and accurate.

Bucktail

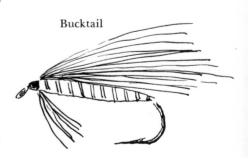

After dark, the fish often continue to feed on spent spinners and the rise form becomes almost unnoticeable. If the moon is out you can wade into position so that the reflection of the moon lines up with the rising trout. On the water you can see tiny dimples which may well be large fish feeding quietly to these spinners. This type of fishing usually does not last longer than an hour but it is very fast and intense—and as it is short lived, it pays to have the right pattern. These fish are aware of the correct size and form because so many of the naturals are passing over their heads. They quickly "get the color," as the English would say. If you think you know what is going on and you have a good pattern and it does not work

Lead-wing Coachman, wet fly

Hare's Ear, wet fly

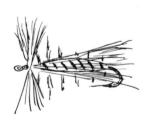

Hair-wing stone fly (dry)

in three or four minutes, check the water with a flashlight and hand net to see what is on the surface. Often the hatch or spinner fall will change just at dusk, as small flies become invisible to the eye. Checking the water is imperative in choosing the correct pattern.

The second type of night fishing is also to actively rising trout and constitutes fishing to a hatch of emerging duns. Some of our largest mayflies, such as the Giant Michigan mayfly of the Midwest, the Brown Drake of the Midwest and West, and also some of our smaller mayflies, such as *Ephemerella dorothea,* later in the season, hatch after dark. Here again, size, shape, and floating ability are usually more important than color, but a good representation of the naturals is necessary. Some of our larger species will start hatching at dark and will hatch on and off all night long. When you know this hatch is in progress do not stop fishing an hour after dark. It is quite possible that you will have spurts of great activity later that night. Extremely large fish will move from their holes and hiding places and range widely over the river. We have seen browns and rainbows move four to five *hundred* feet from their hiding places to feed on these large night-hatching duns.

At night, long, fine leaders are not required, and since fifteen-pound browns are not unheard of at night on large dry flies, it is best to be equipped with large, strong, sharp hooks and the heaviest leaders practical for the size fly you are using. You should check your flies often at night to make sure they have not picked up a small piece of grass and that they are dry and floating well. Sometimes a small tangle can develop in the dark at the end of your leader, which you will be unaware of unless you check periodically. It is usually impossible to tell if your fly is dragging after dark and indeed sometimes it does not seem to matter if the fly drags or not, though often it does and various positions should be tried when fishing to an extremely fine fish.

Large fish can be found at night in some of the most unlikely spots imaginable, particularly the rocky shallows, muddy shallows, and gravel bars. On warm nights, trout often prowl these areas for crayfish, baitfish, large beetles, or anything else that might come their way. This type of fishing is especially good after the spinner fall is over and when no aquatic insects are actually hatching out of the water. It can be effective from dark till dawn. Short, heavy leaders are in order here as large fish are often encountered. The hooks on these flies should be very sharp as large fish often have hard, bony mouths. These large dry flies are cast straight across and then let to swing on a dead drift. Here again, if you wade quietly, long casts are not necessary. Many strikes are missed in this type of fishing by casting downstream at too great an angle; casting at 45° from the trout produces many more hooked fish on the strike. In this type of fishing, if the moon is out, work the dark side of the river in the shadows.

Our favorite types of patterns for this type of fishing are large night moths, either tied with a clipped deer-hair body and impala wings with no hackle, or a night moth with a body of mohlon, a short hackle tied palmer, and a deer hair or impala wing. The two colors of the most common naturals are light cream and brown; fish seem to show a definite preference for the lighter variety. Large salmon-type dry stone flies are often very effective. Many of our streams have large stone flies returning to lay their eggs after dark; often they swim across the water in the expelling operation. The patterns we use are also good imitations of the huge caddis flies that one encounters periodically at night. Often extremely large Western patterns, such as #6 or #8 Irresistibles or Goofus Bugs are good fished in Midwestern and Eastern rivers at night. Usually with this kind of fishing you are covering a lot of water so it is important to know the holes you are fishing. *It is dangerous not to.*

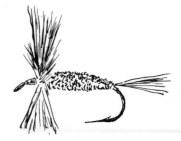

Irresistible dry fly

Another type of night fishing consists of wet-fly and streamer fishing. You can be just under the surface with a floating line or deep with a high-density sinking line. Fur-bodied squirreled tails are effective fished shallow to imitate the nymphs and adults of stone flies, either ready to crawl out of the water to hatch or in the egg-laying process. Large wet flies such as the Gold-Ribbed Hares Ear, and Leadwing Coachman, size #2, #4, #6, and #8 are very effective. These imitate caddis flies and stone flies. A yellow body with a gray-squirrel wing and brown hackle is good, as is an orange body with a fox squirrel wing. Our favorite pattern, however, on which we have caught more large trout at night than any other streamer, is a fox squirrel wing with a red wool body, gold ribbing, and brown hackle. It is best tied in sizes from #2 to #10; the smaller sizes are used at dusk and just before dark and the larger sizes later on as the night progresses. This type of fishing consists mainly of casting slightly down and across stream and letting the streamer either swim dead or drawing it slowly back or striping back as fast as you can. All three methods work well and you must experiment to see which one works best on a particular night. These flies are also fished in deep holes and runs with a high-density line and if the water is extremely fast and deep the flies are weighted.

Grey Ghost streamer

Large bivisible—flying caddis

Remember, many fish will cruise the shallow gravel bars and riffles, sometimes with their dorsal fins and back completely out of the water, grubbing for crawdads that are kicking out of their skins or shells in order to undergo the next growth cycle, much as a mayfly nymph sheds its outer skin many times in order to grow; or they may cruise looking for the minnows and baitfish that inhabit the shallows. The stone-fly nymphs are in the shallows at night on their way to crawl out on the bank to hatch. A light squirrel tail fished with a floating line can often produce explosive action in such places.

A couple more suggestions: fishing blind in shallow water leads to snags, so a fly tied upside down so the hook rides up is a great help. The new keel hooks are very good for night fishing. It is best if you can learn to change flies without the use of a flashlight. Bright light will scare large trout and ruin a good pool for a long time.

Night fishing adds new dimensions to your trout fishing—and it may well be the time you land your largest trout.

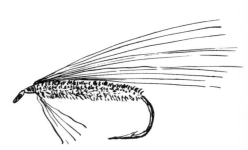

Squirrel-tail streamer

CHAPTER 14

A Barbless Hook

TRADITION IS SOMETHING handed down from the past—an inherited culture, belief, practice, or attitude. Very few fields of endeavor have more tradition associated with them than the sport of fly-fishing. Only in recent years have trends toward significant improvement and advancement been realized. Equipment, for example, has improved tremendously in the past decade, including the development of such items as better-floating and longer-lasting fly lines, glass rods that have outstanding action, and leaders with increased strength and fineness of diameter. Flies are finally being constructed, by at least a few tiers, that are based on common sense, not tradition—and they are much more realistic. In fact, a major theme of this book has been to reexamine the traditional ideas and advance new concepts. If nothing more, we hope we have instilled the idea of using common sense and close observation as criteria for devising effective patterns.

In the modern world we must constantly be prepared to adjust our thinking to cope with changing situations. Other areas of activity, such as business and science, have thrown tradition to the wind in order that progress can be made. There is one facet of our sport where we *must* adjust our thinking and depart from tradition—the choice of killing or releasing. For some illogical reason, an important aspect of our trout-fishing tradition has demanded that we kill our catch. This probably originated with our early forefathers, who had to depend on wildlife for survival. In those days it was a matter of necessity to provide one's own food, shelter, and clothing. Today, this is certainly not the case, yet we seem to possess these same deep-rooted tendencies of our ancestors. Our present-day standard of living hardly requires that we kill our catch for food. If fish is a must in one's diet, it is far cheaper to patronize the local fish market.

Some fishermen who kill their fish feel they are proving their prowess by displaying creels and freezers full of dead fish. Fortunately, people who exhibit this characteristic are, at best, fishermen of mediocre skill. By the time an angler has climbed to higher plateaus, he is aware of what the sport is all about and realizes that his enjoyment comes from the challenge of imitation and appreciation of the environment—*and not from killing trout*. The amount of satisfaction and enjoyment gained is the real measure of success, not how many dead fish can be stacked in a freezer like cordwood. Good fishermen recognize the fact that they can seriously jeopardize their sport and normally make an effort to limit their kill. They realize that the whole idea of fly-fishing is the deception of *live* trout and that by killing their catch they kill their sport. They also realize that each time a trout is released he becomes a little more leader-shy and sophisticated. Trout that are smarter and more sophisticated create a greater challenge for deception, and this, of course, improves our sport. These are the kinds of fish we enjoy fishing over. One of this variety is worth half a dozen fresh out of the hatchery.

With the mounting problems of overpopulation, pollution, and the ever-decreasing amount of good trout water, we must soon make some meaningful decisions concerning our sport. In the end, it pretty much boils down to the choice of fishing with regulations or not fishing at all. On this basis, it's quite obvious what must be done. More stringent size and creel limitations are required generally, while in specific areas no-kill and trophy-fish regulations are needed. For the total picture, what we need is a drastically reduced kill. It sounds like a simple solution and should be, but unfortunately this is not the case. Whenever these recommendations are suggested, an immediate howl goes up from many quarters. Strangely, the people who yell the loudest about poor fishing are the ones who destroy their own sport by killing every fish they catch.

What we need is a new breed of angler who is truly interested in the improvement of our sport—improvement that will come about only when a significantly increased number of fishermen gain greater knowledge and insight. Education and enlightenment separate the true anglers—who limit

their kill—from those who kill their limit. We must all work through any means at our disposal to promote and improve the quality of fly-fishing everywhere. Various groups, such as sportsmen's clubs, fly-fishing federations, and fly-tying organizations, provide excellent mediums through which information can be assembled and properly transmitted to the uninformed. These groups should also work closely with the state conservation departments to promote necessary regulations that will insure the quality fly-fishing we all desire.

The future of our sport is contingent upon our ability to reverse present trends of stream pollution, dam building, liberal regulations, and uneducated anglers. Reversal of these prevailing tendencies will come about only through the organized actions of aroused and concerned individuals. Since fly-fishermen represent a distinct minority group, the best procedure is to sell clean water to the public rather than to promote trout fishing only. The great dam builders can best be regulated by putting pressure on our legislators, both state and federal. As for regulations, our conservation agencies must be influenced and convinced that "harvest" does not necessarily mean *dead fish*. Harvest also means "a reward for exertion," and what better reward is there for the true angler than a released *live* trout that is free to rise again? Similar concepts must be advanced to the uneducated angler in such a manner that he will eventually realize that it takes a far bigger and better man to release a trout than to kill one. Perhaps it can all start for *you* with a barbless hook.

Selected Bibliography

BERGMAN, RAY. *Trout*. New York: Alfred A. Knopf, Inc., 1938; second edition, 1965.

BLADES, WILLIAM F. *Fishing Flies and Fly Tying*. Harrisburg: The Stackpole Company, 1951.

BURKS, B. D. *The Mayflies, or Ephemeroptera, of Illinois*. University of Illinois, Natural History Survey, 1953.

DUNNE, J. W. *Sunshine and the Dry Fly*. London: A. C. Black, Ltd.: 1924.

EDMUNDS, F. GEORGE, JR. *Mayflies of Utah* (Ephemeroptera). University of Massachusetts, 1952. Unpublished doctoral thesis.

FLICK, ART. *Streamside Guide to Naturals and Their Imitations*. New York: G. P. Putnam's Sons, 1947; Crown Publishers, Inc., 1970.

GODDARD, JOHN. *Trout Fly Recognition*. London: A. C. Black, Ltd., 1966.

HARRIS, J. R. *An Angler's Entomology*. South Brunswick: A. S. Barnes and Co., 1952.

JENNINGS, PRESTON J. *A Book of Trout Flies*. New York: The Derrydale Press, 1935; Crown Publishers, Inc., 1970.

JENSEN, STEVEN. *Mayflies of Idaho*. Unpublished Master's Thesis, University of Utah.

LEONARD, J. EDSON. *Flies*. South Brunswick: A. S. Barnes, Inc., 1950.

LEONARD, JUSTIN W. and FANNIE A. *Mayflies of Michigan Trout Streams*. Bloomfield Hills: Cranbrook Institute of Science, 1962.

MARINARO, VINCENT C. *A Modern Dry-Fly Code*. New York: G. P. Putnam's Sons, 1950; Crown Publishers, Inc., 1970.

NEEDHAM, JAMES G., TRAVER, J. R., and HSU, YIN CHI. *Biology of Mayflies*. Ithaca: Comstock, 1935.

QUICK, JIM. *Fishing the Nymph*. New York: The Ronald Press, 1960.

RHEAD, LOUIS. *American Trout Stream Insects*. New York: Frederick A. Stokes Co., 1916.

SCHWIEBERT, ERNEST G. *Matching the Hatch*. New York: The Macmillan Company, 1955.

USINGER, ROBERT L. *Aquatic Insects of California*. Berkeley and Los Angeles: University of California Press, 1918.

The Identification of Mayflies

KNOWLEDGE OF THE scientific classification of mayflies can be extremely beneficial to the trout fisherman; for it will aid in streamside identification and recognition. Often the ability to establish the identity of an insect will allow the angler an opportunity to fish the hatch in accordance with the emerging and/or egg-laying characteristics of the natural. Nymphs of the same family and genus are normally similar in shape and form and, once familiar with them, can be identified at a glance. Identification of the species, however, can be much more difficult. Some are easily recognized, but often an entomologist is required to differentiate between the various species of the same genus. Familiarity with the general form of families and genera is invaluable in determining the types of hatches on a given river. The following pages will help in distinguishing nymph and adult forms and characteristics.

Many fishermen will not desire to learn the true names of the hatches that they fish, but usage of the correct names is the best way of passing on knowledge and new developments. This country has such a large number of species that common names merely create confusion. For example, the

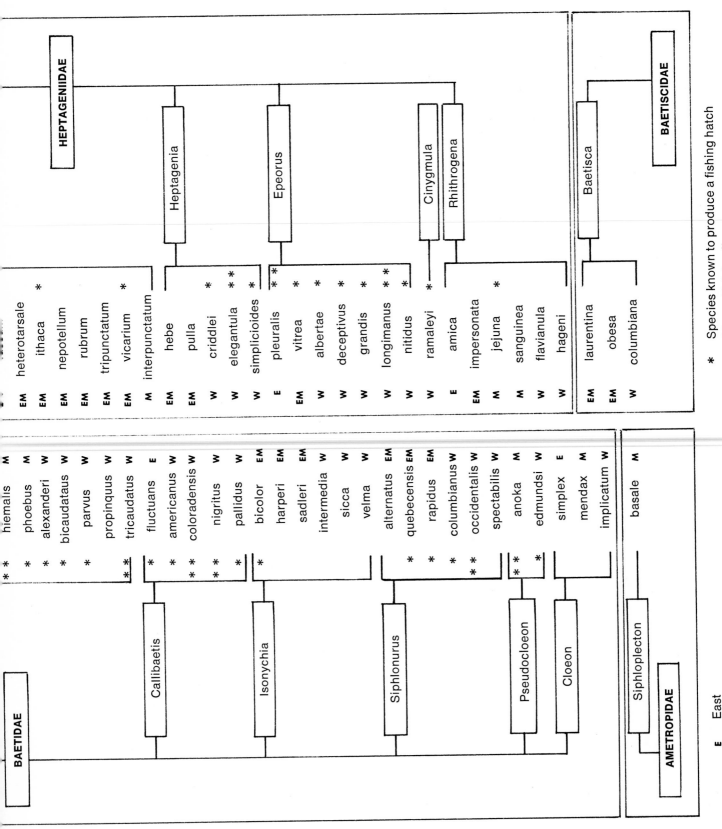

HEPTAGENIIDAE

Heptagenia
- EM heterotarsale
- EM ithaca *
- EM nepotellum
- EM rubrum
- EM tripunctatum
- EM vicarium *
- M interpunctatum
- EM hebe
- EM pulla
- W criddlei *
- W elegantula **
- W simplicioides *

Epeorus
- E pleuralis **
- EM vitrea *
- W albertae *
- W deceptivus *
- W grandis *
- W longimanus **
- W nitidus *

Cinygmula
- W ramaleyi *

Rhithrogena
- W amica
- EM impersonata
- E jejuna *
- M sanguinea
- W flavianula
- W hageni

BAETISCIDAE

Baetisca
- EM laurentina
- EM obesa
- W columbiana

BAETIDAE

Callibaetis
- ** M hiemalis
- * M phoebus
- * W alexanderi
- * W bicaudataus
- * W parvus
- W propinquus
- ** W tricaudatus

Isonychia
- * E fluctuans
- * W americanus
- ** W coloradensis
- ** W nigritus
- W pallidus

Siphlonurus
- * EM bicolor
- EM harperi
- EM sadleri
- W intermedia
- W sicca
- W velma
- * EM alternatus
- * EM quebecensis
- ** EM rapidus

Pseudocloeon
- ** W columbianus
- * W occidentalis
- W spectabilis

Cloeon
- M anoka
- W edmundsi
- E simplex
- M mendax
- W implicatum

AMETROPIDAE

Siphloplecton
- M basale

* Species known to produce a fishing hatch

** "Super Hatches"

E   East

M   Midwest

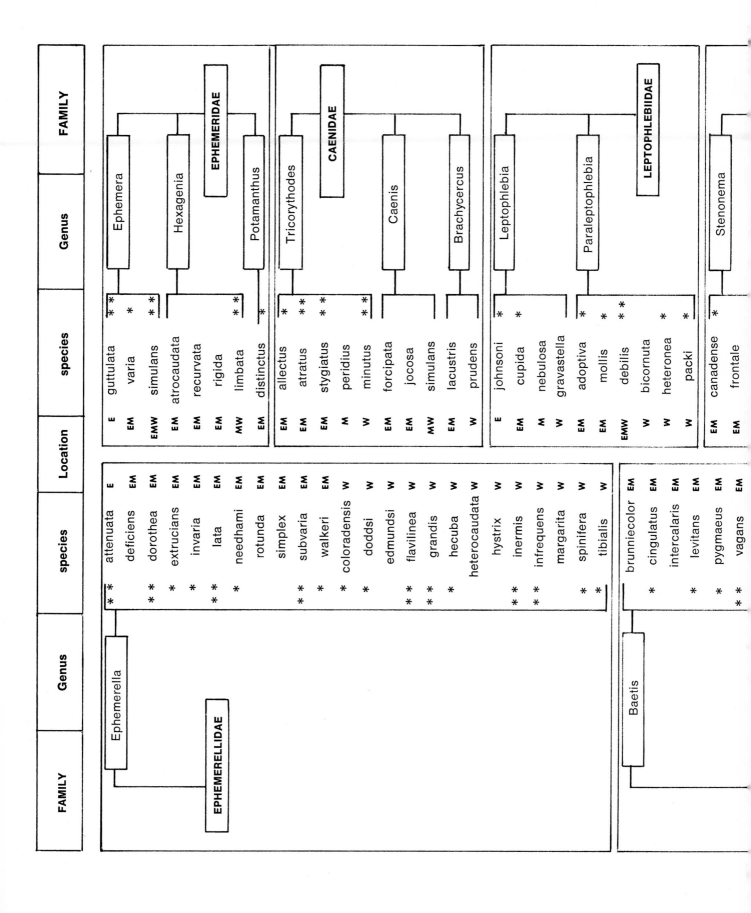

FAMILY	Genus	species	Location
EPHEMERIDAE	Ephemera	guttulata *	E
		varia *	EM
		simulans **	EMW
	Hexagenia	atrocaudata	EM
		recurvata	EM
		rigida	EM
		limbata **	MW
	Potamanthus	distinctus *	EM
CAENIDAE	Tricorythodes	allectus *	EM
		atratus **	EM
		stygiatus **	EM
		peridius	M
		minutus **	W
	Caenis	forcipata	EM
		jocosa	EM
		simulans	MW
		lacustris	W
	Brachycercus	prudens	W
LEPTOPHLEBIIDAE	Leptophlebia	johnsoni *	E
		cupida *	EM
		nebulosa	M
		gravastella	W
	Paraleptophlebia	adoptiva *	EM
		mollis *	EM
		debilis **	EMW
		bicornuta	W
		heteronea *	W
		packi *	W
	Stenonema	canadense *	EM
		frontale	EM

FAMILY	Genus	species	Location
EPHEMERELLIDAE	Ephemerella	attenuata **	E
		deficiens **	EM
		dorothea *	EM
		extrucians **	EM
		invaria **	EM
		lata	EM
		needhami *	EM
		rotunda	EM
		simplex **	EM
		subvaria **	EM
		walkeri *	EM
		coloradensis *	W
		doddsi *	W
		edmundsi	W
		flavilinea	W
		grandis **	W
		hecuba **	W
		heterocaudata *	W
		hystrix	W
		inermis	W
		infrequens **	W
		margarita	W
		spinifera *	W
		tibialis *	W
	Baetis	brunniecolor	EM
		cingulatus *	EM
		intercalaris	EM
		levitans *	EM
		pygmaeus *	EM
		vagans **	EM

Hendrickson of the East is called the Borchers Drake in the Midwest, yet both are the same fly, *Ephemerella subvaria.* There are at least twenty mayflies which could be called Blue-wing Olives. A Western angler may learn that the nymph of "his" Pale Evening Dun emerges underwater and so informs his Eastern friend. This could be a very valuable piece of information, as an emerging pattern should be deadly, but the Pale Evening Dun of the West is not the same fly the Eastern friend is thinking of, so to him the information is worse than useless, and may even be confusing. The only way one can really communicate is to use the true or scientific names. So for those of you who wish to use them, the information detailed in this appendix should be useful.

All living things are classified as either plant or animal. All members of the plant and animal kingdom are classified under categories which represent relationships to each other. An example, *Ephemera guttulata,* the Green Drake, one of our most important Eastern trout stream mayflies, is as follows:

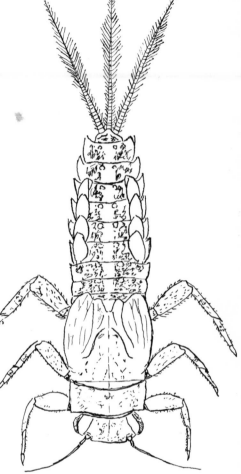

Kingdom: Animal (all animal life)
Subkingdom: Invertebrate (all animals without backbones)
Phylum: Arthropoda (all animals with external skeletons, bilateral symmetry, jointed legs)
Class: Insecta (all true insects)
Order: Ephemeroptera (all mayflies)
Family: Ephemeridae (all true burrowing mayflies)
Genus: *Ephemera* (a group of a few closely related kinds of burrowing mayflies)
Species: *guttulata* (a particular kind of burrowing mayfly)

This chart illustrates the families and their corresponding genera and species of the trout-stream insects of North America, including East, Midwest, and West. All these mayflies will be found in trout streams, although not all will hatch in numbers to cause a rise of trout. The species which we know produce a fishing hatch are marked (+) and the ones that produce what we call "superhatches" are marked (++). Undoubtedly some others not marked do also, but we have not encountered them. There are many other warm water species, but since they will not be seen on trout streams they are not included here. Following the chart is information on each family, including only the genera and species that are of importance to the angler. The species of each genus are listed in charts which contain such data as common names, size, water type, emergence dates, hatch time, spinner fall, and a general description of all three stages. Line drawings of nymph forms and other characteristics are also included.

Ephemerella inermis

EPHEMERELLIDAE

This family contains but one genus, *Ephemerella,* which is undoubtedly one of the most important genera of mayflies.

EPHEMERELLA

Members of this genus are found in great abundance and occupy a wide variety of habitats. *Ephemerella subvaria* starts the season in April, with other species hatching continuously until October. Due to their manner of emergence, most species are extremely vulnerable to the trout. At hatch time, the nymphs leave the bottom and rise to the surface. Normally, the subimagos emerge from the nymphal skin several inches below the film, making the emerging pattern a very deadly imitation. Once on the surface, the floating duns often require thirty to sixty seconds to get airborne. Members of this genus are similar in outline and appearance, and once familiar with them, they can be recognized at a glance. The various species of Ephemerella are sometimes similar, but knowledge of the minor differences can be valuable to the angler.

Ephemerella nymphs vary widely as to body shape and form. Some are

STRUCTURE OF GENERALIZED MAYFLY NYMPHS

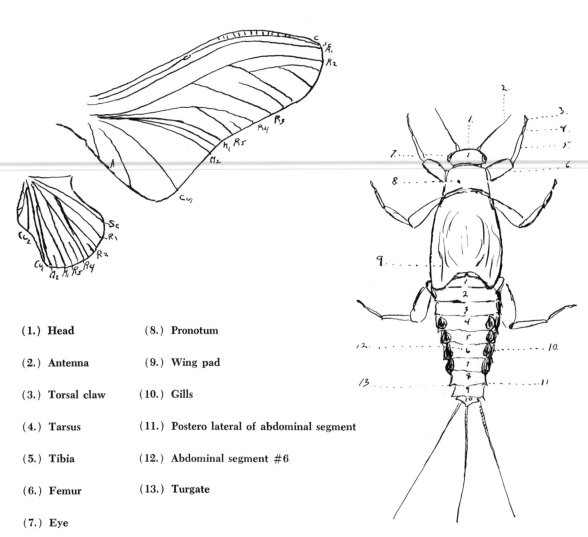

(1.) Head

(2.) Antenna

(3.) Torsal claw

(4.) Tarsus

(5.) Tibia

(6.) Femur

(7.) Eye

(8.) Pronotum

(9.) Wing pad

(10.) Gills

(11.) Postero lateral of abdominal segment

(12.) Abdominal segment #6

(13.) Turgate

fairly slender and streamlined, while others have flattened bodies and legs. Some species are smooth, some have conspicuous projections or spines, and others are covered with fine hairs. Dorsal platelike gills are present on segments 3 to 7 in many species, but on 4 to 7 in a few others. In the latter situation, the gills of segment 4 are sometimes enlarged and lidlike, concealing most or all of the other gills. Nymphs have three equal tails that are normally about the length of the body and are often hairy. Mayflies of this genus vary greatly as to size, ranging from 4 to 15 mm in body length. The subimagos are quite variable in coloration and markings, but most imagos display shades of brown or olive. Eyes of the female are small and located on the sides of the head, while those of the male are much larger, normally meeting on top of the head. All tarsi are four-jointed, except in the foreleg of the male, which has 5 segments. Three tails of approximately equal length are retained in the adult stage.

STRUCTURE OF GENERALIZED MAYFLY, ADULT MALE

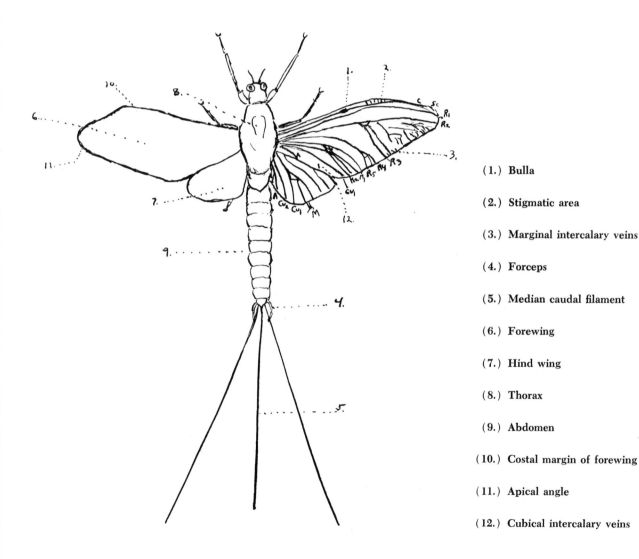

(1.) Bulla

(2.) Stigmatic area

(3.) Marginal intercalary veins

(4.) Forceps

(5.) Median caudal filament

(6.) Forewing

(7.) Hind wing

(8.) Thorax

(9.) Abdomen

(10.) Costal margin of forewing

(11.) Apical angle

(12.) Cubical intercalary veins

	Common Name	Locality	Size in mm	Water type	Emergence	Hatch Time	Spinner Fall	Body of Dun	Wing of Dun	Body of Spinner	Wing of Spinner	Body of Nymph	Tails N	D	S
subvaria	Hendrickson	E M	9–12	fast to medium	Apr. 25 to June 15	afternoon	evening or afternoon	brownish olive and yellow	slate	reddish brown	hyaline	dark brown	3	3	3
invaria	Hendrickson	E M	7–9	fast to medium	May 5 to July 20	afternoon	evening or afternoon	brownish olive and yellow	slate	reddish brown	hyaline	brown, light marks	3	3	3
rotunda	Hendrickson	E M	7–9	fast to medium	May 7 to June 10	afternoon	evening or afternoon	brownish olive and yellow	slate	reddish brown	hyaline	yellowish brown	3	3	3
dorothea	Sulphur	E M	6–9	fast to medium	May 15 to July 5	afternoon and evening	evening	yellow, yellow orange	light yellowish gray	yellowish brown	hyaline	yellowish brown	3	3	3
lata	Slate-wing Olive	E M	6–8	fast to medium	July 1 to Aug. 10	morning	evening	olive green	dark slate	brown or olive	hyaline	dark brown	3	3	3
excrucians	Blue-wing Olive	E M	5–6	fast to medium	June 10 to June 25	afternoon and evening	evening	brownish olive	light gray	brown	hyaline	dark grayish brown	3	3	3
attenuata	Slate-wing Olive	E	6–9	fast to medium	June 5 to July 5	sporadic	sporadic	light olive	dark slate	brown	hyaline	medium brown	3	3	3
walkeri	Slate Drake	E M	8–10	fast to medium	July 26 to Aug. 20	sporadic	sporadic	blackish olive	dark slate	brown	hyaline	medium brown	3	3	3
needhami	Red Quill	E M	6–8	fast to medium	June 20 to July 20	evening	evening	brownish olive	black	brown	hyaline	light and dark brown	3	3	3
inermis	Pale Morning Dun—#2	W	5–7	slow to fast	July 1 to Aug. 30	midday	morning and evening	yellow, olive cast	light gray	yellowish olive	hyaline	dark olive brown	3	3	3

	Common Name	Locality	Size in mm	Water type	Emergence	Hatch Time	Spinner Fall	Body of Dun	Wing of Dun	Body of Spinner	Wing of Spinner	Body of Nymph	Tails N D S
grandis	Western Green Drake	W	14–16	slow to medium	June 15 to July 15	midday	night	green with dark brown rings	slate	brown	hyaline	dark brown	3 3 3
hecuba	Great Red Quill	W	14–16	slow to medium	July 1 to Aug. 30	midday	evening	light tan, dark brown marks	gray	reddish brown	hyaline	brown, mottled	3 3 3
coloradensis		W	12–13	fast to medium	July 1 to Oct. 15	midday	evening	brownish olive, dark brown marks	gray	dark brown	hyaline	brown, mottled	3 3 3
flavilinea	Slate-wing Olive	W	8–10	medium	June 25 to Aug. 20	evening	morning and evening	greenish olive	slate	light reddish brown	hyaline	dark brown	3 3 3
doddsi		W	13–14	fast to medium	July 1 to Aug. 30	midday	evening	brownish olive, dark marks	gray	reddish brown	hyaline	yellow, tan	3 3 3
spinifera		W	11–12	fast to medium	July 1 to Oct. 15	midday	morning and dusk	brown, light olive under	medium gray	brown	hyaline	reddish brown	3 3 3
tibialis		W	7–8	fast to medium	June 1 to Oct. 15	midday	dusk	dark reddish brown	light gray	purplish brown	hyaline	blackish brown	3 3 3
infrequens	Pale Morning Dun—#3	W	7–9	medium	July 1 to Oct. 15	midday	morning and evening	yellow, olive cast	yellowish gray	brown	hyaline	dark brown	3 3 3
lacustris	Pale Morning Dun—#1	W	7–9	slow	June 5 to July 30	morning	morning and evening	yellow, olive cast	yellowish gray	greenish tan	hyaline	dark brown	3 3 3

BAETIDAE

The genera of Baetidae that are of importance to the angler include *Baetis, Callibaetis, Isonychia, Siphlonurus, Pseudocloeon,* and *Cloeon.* The mayflies of this family vary greatly in size, ranging from the tiny #24 *Pseudocloeons* to the #10 species of *Siphlonurus* and *Isonychia.* Nymphs are similar, being streamlined and able to swim swiftly, however, the adults are more varied.

BAETIS

This genus is significant all year long but is especially important from mid-summer to late fall when the larger flies are scarce. *Baetis* is represented in all sections of the country by a great number of species, all small in size, varying from 4 to 10 mm in length. Nymphs are highly streamlined with long, slender legs and single platelike gills on segments 1 to 7. Some species have only two tails, but most have three, with the middle one distinctly shorter. Adults have paired marginal veinlets in the fore wing, tiny hind wings, with a hooklike projection on the front edge, and two tails. Eyes of the male are turbinate.

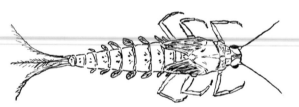

Baetis hiemalis

155

	Common Name	Locality	Size in mm	Water type	Emergence	Hatch Time	Spinner Fall	Body of Dun	Wing of Dun	Body of Spinner	Wing of Spinner	Body of Nymph	Tails N	D	S
vagans	Blue-wing Olive	E M	6–7	medium	Apr. 15 to Aug. 25	noon, evening	morning	brownish olive	slate	brownish olive	hyaline	olive brown	3	2	2
levitans	Blue-wing Olive	E M	4–5	slow to medium	May 15 to Aug. 25	afternoon and evening	evening	olive	medium gray	brown, segments 2–6 white	hyaline	pale brown	3	2	2
cingulatus	Blue-wing Olive	E M	5–6	medium to fast	May 15 to Aug. 25	afternoon and evening	evening	olive brown	light gray	brown, segments 2–6 white	hyaline	medium olive brown	3	2	2
heimalis	Blue-wing Olive	M	9–10	slow	Sept. 10 to Oct. 5	afternoon	late afternoon	brown	slate	dark blackish brown	hyaline	dark olive	3	2	2
phoebus	Blue-wing Olive	M	5–6	medium	May 10 to June 5	afternoon	evening	olive brown	light gray	brown, segments 2–6 white	hyaline	medium olive brown	3	2	2
pygmaeus	Blue-wing Olive	E M	4–5	slow	Aug. 1 to Sept. 20	afternoon	evening	medium olive	medium gray	dark brown	hyaline	dark brown	3	2	2
tricaudatus	Blue-wing Olive	W	7	slow to fast	April 1 to Oct. 30	sporadic, daylight	early morning and evening	light brown	light gray	dark brown	hyaline	medium olive brown	3	2	2
parvus	Blue-wing Olive	W	5–6	medium	May 1 to Sept. 25	sporadic, daylight	early morning and evening	dark olive brown	dark gray	brown, segments 2–6 white	hyaline	dark olive brown	3	2	2
bicaudatus	Blue-wing Olive	W	4–5	medium to fast	April 1 to Oct. 30	sporadic, daylight	early morning and evening	light reddish brown	light gray	reddish brown	hyaline	medium brown	2	2	2
alexanderi	Blue-wing Olive	W	5–6	medium	May 1 to Sept. 30	sporadic, daylight	early morning and evening	light reddish brown	light gray	medium reddish brown	hyaline	medium brown	3	2	2

CALLIBAETIS

Members of this genus are primarily lake dwellers, but two cold water species, *nigritus* and *coloradensis,* are especially important in the West. Nymphs are small to medium in size, have three tails equal in length and rather large heart-shaped gills, which are double on segments 1–6, or 1–7. The outstanding feature of the adults is the freckled appearance of their bodies. Wings of the female have brown markings on the leading edge and both sexes have two tails.

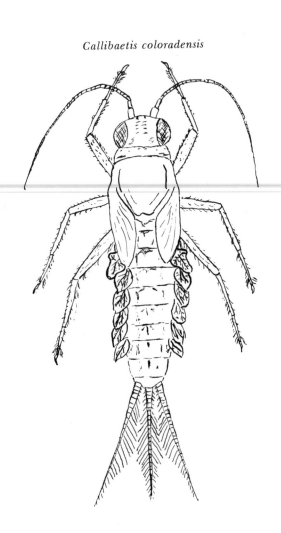

Callibaetis coloradensis

	Common Name	Locality	Size in mm	Water type	Emergence	Hatch Time	Spinner Fall	Body of Dun	Wing of Dun	Body of Spinner	Wing of Spinner	Body of Nymph	Tails N	D	S
fluctuans	Speckled Dun and Spinner	E	6–7	dead to slow	May 15 to June 20	sporadic	sporadic	olive brown	gray, dark marks	brownish white	hyaline, brown veins	brown	3	2	2
nigritus	Speckled Dun and Spinner	W	9–12	dead to slow	May 1 to Nov. 15	dusk	morning and dusk	tannish olive	gray, white veins	tannish gray, speckled	hyaline, brownish marks	grayish brown	3	2	2
coloradensis	Speckled Dun and Spinner	W	9–12	dead to slow	June 20 to Sept. 30	afternoon	morning and dusk	tannish	slate, white veins	tannish gray, speckled	hyaline, brownish marks	grayish brown	3	2	2
americanus	Speckled Dun and Spinner	W	7–8	dead to slow	July 20 to Aug. 10	sporadic	sporadic	gray, brown rings	gray, white veins	tannish gray, speckled	hyaline, brownish marks	grayish brown	3	2	2
pallidus	Speckled Dun and Spinner	W	8–9	dead to slow	Aug. 20 to Sept. 15	sporadic	sporadic	light tan	pale yellow	brown with light rings	hyaline	grayish brown	3	2	2

ISONYCHIA

Only one species, *bicolor,* will be described as all others are very similar in appearance. Nymphs are large and streamlined and have three tails, the middle one fringed on both sides and the lateral ones on the inner margins only. Thick fringes of hair are borne on the inner side of the forelegs, while the fore tibia bears a conspicuous spine. Adults are usually reddish brown to purplish brown in color, with the forelegs being brown and the middle and hind legs being pale or whitish.

Isonychia bicolor

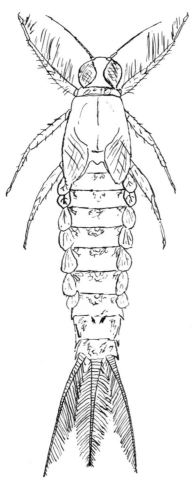

Common Name	Locality	Size in mm	Water type	Emergence	Hatch Time	Spinner Fall	Body of Dun	Wing of Dun	Body of Spinner	Wing of Spinner	Body of Nymph	Tails N D S
bicolor												
Large Mahogany Dun	E M	13–16	fast	May 20 to Sept. 20	afternoon and evening	evening	dark reddish brown	dark slate	reddish brown	hyaline	dark brown	3 2 2

	Locality	Common Name	Size in mm	Water type	Emergence	Hatch Time	Spinner Fall	Body of Dun	Wing of Dun	Body of Spinner	Wing of Spinner	Body of Nymph	Tails N	D	S
rapidus	E M	Gray Drake	9–12	slow	May 25 to June 20	sporadic	evening	purplish gray	brownish gray	grayish brown	hyaline	dark olive	3	2	2
quebecensis	E M	Gray Drake	14–16	slow	May 20 to June 30	sporadic	evening	purplish gray	brownish gray	grayish brown	hyaline	dark olive	3	2	2
columbianus	W	Gray Drake	12–13	slow	June 15 to Aug. 30	sporadic	morning and evening	gray, brown rings	slate	gray, brown rings	hyaline	gray brown	3	2	2
occidentalis	W	Drake	12–15	slow	Aug. 10 to Oct. 10	midday	morning and evening	gray, brown rings	slate	grayish brown, light rings	hyaline	brownish gray	3	2	2

SIPHLONURUS

Members of this genus form the Gray Drake hatch in Michigan and are known as Dark Gray Drakes in the West. The nymphs of *Siphlonurus* are streamlined, medium to large in size and have platelike gills that are all similar in shape. Tails are fringed the same as *Isonychia* nymphs. Adult fore wings are long in relation to their width and the hind wings are well developed. Both male and female are similar in coloration, being conspicuously marked with various shades of purplish gray and reddish brown. As in *Isonychia*, two tails are present in the adult stage.

Siphlonurus

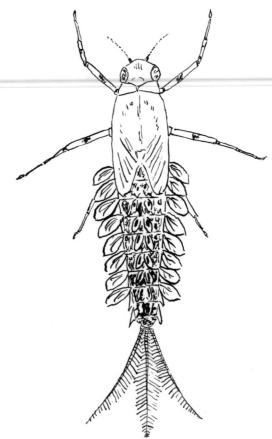

PSEUDOCLOEON

These are very tiny mayflies, ranging from 4 to 6 mm, with the nymphs a little stockier than those of *Baetis*. They also differ from *Baetis* nymphs by having only two tails and lacking hind wing pads. Gills are single on all segments. Adults have one pair of wings, which possess paired marginal veinlets, and two tails.

Locality	Common Name	Size in mm	Water type	Emergence	Hatch Time	Spinner Fall	Body of Dun	Wing of Dun	Body of Spinner	Wing of Spinner	Body of Nymph	Tails N D S
anoka M	Tiny Blue-wing Olive	4–5	slow to medium	June 20 to Sept. 30	sporadic and evening	evening	olive	light gray	olive, rusty olive	hyaline	olive	2 2 2
edmundsi W	Tiny Blue-wing Olive	4–5	slow to medium	July 1 to Sept. 30	sporadic and evening	evening	olive	light gray	light brown	hyaline	olive	2 2 2

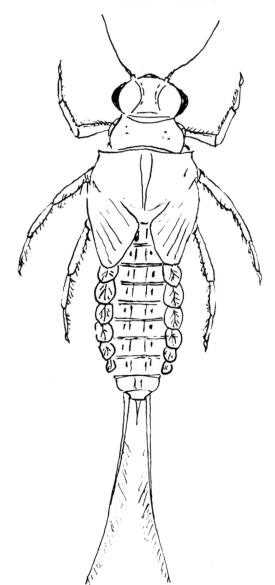

Pseudocloeon anoka

CLOEON

Only one species, *implicatum,* will be described for this genus. Nymphs have double gills on all segments, or on segments 1 to 6. They also have three tails and lack hind wing pads. Adults only have two tails and one pair of wings that exhibit single marginal veinlets.

AMETROPIDAE

This family contains only one genus, *Siphloplecton,* that we have found to be significant to the fly-fisherman. The nymphs are large and streamlined, similar to *Siphlonurus,* but are readily distinguished by their long claws.

Siphloplecton

These are rather large mayflies, ranging from 12 to 18 mm in length. In the nymph, claws of the middle and hind legs are almost as long as the tarsus, while the front claws are shorter and forked. Three conspicuous stripes are located on the undersurface of the abdomen. The three tails are equal in length, with the middle one bearing long hairs on both sides and the outer ones bearing hair on the inner margins only. An outstanding feature of the adults are the heavily spotted fore wings, which are nearly three times as long as wide and contain two pairs of cubital intercalary veins. Adults have three tails and are generally brownish in coloration.

BAETISCIDAE

This family contains but one genus, *Baetisca,* which, to our knowledge, does not create a hatch of any significance to the angler. It is included for identification purposes only.

BAETISCA

The unique appearance of the nymph is strikingly different from any other genera. They possess a large carapace or shieldlike structure which completely covers the upper surface of the thorax and abdominal segments 1 to 5. The three tails are very short and approximately equal in length. Both carapace and head exhibit hornlike projections. Adults are characterized by a thorax that is unusually large and an abdomen that tapers sharply in its rear half. The middle tail is very short and the hind wings are almost circular in shape.

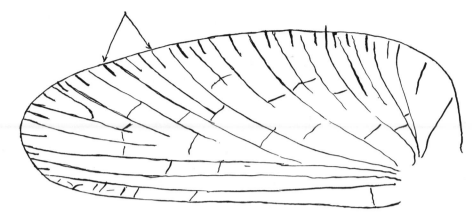

Cloeon—wing showing single marginal veinlets

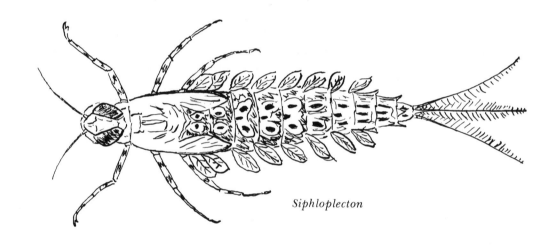

Siphloplecton

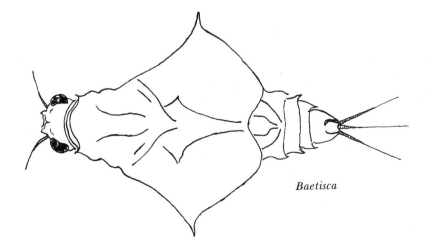

Baetisca

	Common Name	Locality	Size in mm	Water type	Emergence	Hatch Time	Spinner Fall	Body of Dun	Wing of Dun	Body of Spinner	Wing of Spinner	Body of Nymph	Tails N	D	S
implicatum	Tiny Blue-wing Olive	W	8	slow to medium	July 1 to Sept. 30	sporadic and evening	evening	olive	light gray	olive brown	hyaline	olive	3	2	2

HEPTAGENIIDAE

Five genera, *Stenonema, Heptagenia, Epeorus, Cinygmula,* and *Rhithrogena,* are important to the angler and belong to this family. The nymphs are sprawling forms with bodies, legs, and heads that are strongly flattened. As compared to other families, the head is large in relation to the body. Eyes are also large and located on the dorsal surface of the head. Gills are present on abdominal segments 1 to 7. All adults have two tails and five freely movable joints in the hind tarsus. Two parallel pairs of cubital intercalary veins are present in the fore wings, while both fore and hind wings display heavy venation. The males have large spherical eyes that are normally light in coloration during the day and black at night.

STENONEMA

Species of this genus range in size from 6 to 16 mm and are much more common to the East and Midwest; there are practically none in the West. Both the nymphs and adults of individual species vary considerably in coloration, making identification extremely difficult. Nymphs can best be recognized by the fact that gills on segments 1 to 6 are platelike, while the seventh pair is slender and threadlike. Adults are much more difficult to separate and usually require close examination under the microscope.

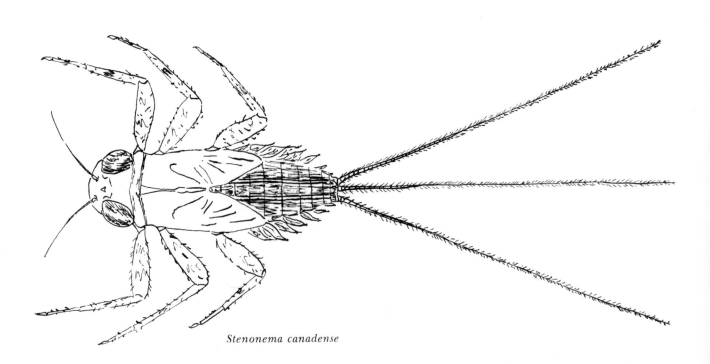

Stenonema canadense

	Common Name	Locality	Size in mm	Water type	Emergence	Hatch Time	Spinner Fall	Body of Dun	Wing of Dun	Body of Spinner	Wing of Spinner	Body of Nymph	Tails N	D	S
canadense	Light Cahill	E M	10–12	fast to medium	June 15 to July 15	sporadic	evening	cream, yellowish olive	cream, brown marks	cream to orange	hyaline, black flecks	brown, light under	3	2	2
ithaca	Light Cahill	E M	10–12	fast to medium	June 20 to July 10	evening	evening	olive brown	olive, brown marks	olive brown	hyaline, black flecks	brown, light under	3	2	2
fuscum	Grey Fox	E M	9–12	fast to medium	May 10 to July 15	sporadic	sporadic	olive brown	olive, brown marks	olive brown	hyaline, black flecks	brown, light under	3	2	2
vicarium	March Brown	E M	10–16	solw to medium	May 20 to June 25	sporadic and evening	evening	olive brown	olive, brown marks	olive brown	hyaline, black flecks	brown, light under	3	2	2
frontale	Light Cahill	E M	8–10	fast to medium	June 10 to Aug. 25	sporadic and evening	evening	pale yellowish olive	cream, brown flecks	cream	hyaline, black flecks	brown, light under	3	2	2
interpunctatum	Light Cahill	M	8–10	fast to medium	July 5 to Aug. 15	sporadic and evening	evening	pale yellowish cream	cream, brown flecks	cream	hyaline, black flecks	brown, light under	3	2	2
heterotarsale	Light Cahill	E M	8–10	fast to medium	June 20 to Aug. 25	sporadic and evening	evening	pale yellowish green	cream, brown flecks	cream	hyaline, black flecks	brown, light under	3	2	2

HEPTAGENIA

Members of this genus are more important to Western anglers than those of the East and Midwest. Species are of variable size, ranging from 4 to 12 mm. Nymphs have three tails and plate-like gills on abdominal segments 1 to 7, which do not extend beneath the body. Adults must be separated by using the keys.

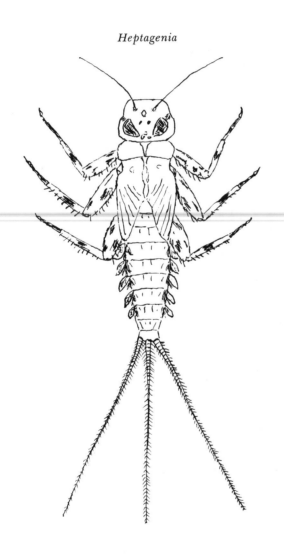

Heptagenia

	Common Name	Locality	Size in mm	Water type	Emergence	Hatch Time	Spinner Fall	Body of Dun	Wing of Dun	Body of Spinner	Wing of Spinner	Body of Nymph	Tails N	D	S
criddlei		W	7	fast to slow	June 10 to July 15	sporadic	morning and evening	brown	gray	gray	hyaline	brown	3	2	2
simplicioides		W	10–12	slow to medium	June 20 to Aug. 20	sporadic	morning and evening	pale cream	light gray	yellowish cream	hyaline	brown	3	2	2
elegantula	Slate-gray Dun	W	9–10	slow to medium	Aug. 5 to Sept. 25	morning	evening	grayish olive with brown rings	dark gray	brownish yellow	hyaline	grayish brown	3	2	2

EPEORUS

Various species of this genus create some of the better hatches of the season in the East and West. These flies are in the 7- to 11-mm size range. Nymphs can easily be differentiated from those of other family members by their possession of only two tails. In the adult stage, the first segment of the fore tarsus is as long as or longer than the second.

Epeorus

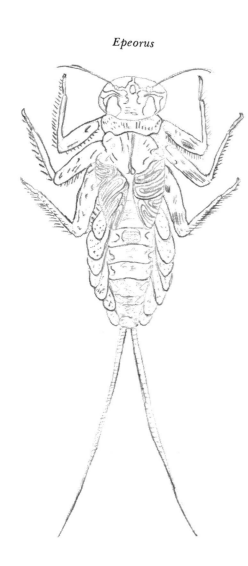

	Common Name	Locality	Size in mm	Water type	Emergence	Hatch Time	Spinner Fall	Body of Dun	Wing of Dun	Body of Spinner	Wing of Spinner	Body of Nymph	Tails N D S
pleuralis	Quill Gordon	E	9–11	fast	Apr. 20 to May 20	afternoon	midday	yellowish with brown markings	slate	yellowish with brown markings	hyaline	dark grayish brown	2 2 2
vitrea	Pale Evening Dun	E M	9–11	fast	May 20 to July 15	evening	evening	pale olive yellow	light gray	yellowish cream	hyaline	grayish brown	2 2 2
albertae	Slate-cream Dun	W	9–10	medium to fast	July 5 to Aug. 15	evening	morning and evening	grayish pink, brown marking	slate	cream	hyaline	grayish brown	2 2 2
longimanus	Slate-brown Dun	W	10–11	fast	June 15 to July 15	morning	afternoon	gray, brown rings	slate	reddish brown to pale brown	hyaline	mottled brown	2 2 2
nitidus	Slate-maroon Dun	W	9–12	fast	June 1 to July 15	morning	evening	top brown, maroon under	slate	reddish brown	hyaline	mottled brown	2 2 2
grandis	Great Red Quill	W	9–12	fast	July 1 to Aug. 30	sporadic	evening	dark brown	slate	reddish brown	hyaline	mottled brown	2 2 2
deceptivus		W	8–9	medium	July 1 to Oct. 20	sporadic	evening	yellow	tannish gray	light brown	hyaline	mottled brown	2 2 2

CINYGMULA

Members of this genus are relatively uniform in size, ranging from 7 to 9 mm in body length. They are common mainly in the West and only one species, *ramaleyi*, seems to be of importance. Gills are present on segments 1 to 7 of the nymph, with the gills of segment 1 being heart shaped and larger than the others. Adults are difficult to separate, requiring the use of the keys.

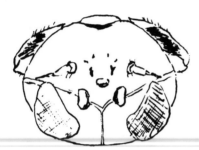

Head of Cinygmula nymph, top view

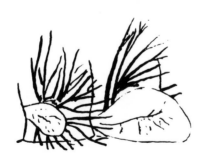

Side view of abdominal segments, showing gills 1 and 2

	Locality	Common Name	Size in mm	Water type	Emergence	Hatch Time	Spinner Fall	Body of Dun	Wing of Dun	Body of Spinner	Wing of Spinner	Body of Nymph	Tails N	D	S
ramaleyi	W	Dark Red Quill	8	fast	May 25 to June 30	sporadic	sporadic	reddish brown, ringed	slate	reddish brown	hyaline, amber tint	dark, reddish brown	3	2	2

RHITHROGENA

The nymphs of this genus are the only ones in the family that possess enlarged gill plates, which extend under the body to form a suctionlike device. Adults tend to be dark brown or reddish brown in color and have crossveins in the stigmatic area of the wing that are interjoined into a network.

Rhithrogena

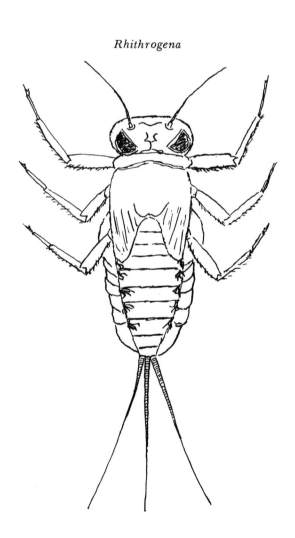

species	Common Name	Locality	Size in mm	Water type	Emergence	Hatch Time	Spinner Fall	Body of Dun	Wing of Dun	Body of Spinner	Wing of Spinner	Body of Nymph	Tails N	D	S
jejuna	Red Quill	M	8–9	fast	May 5 to June 5	afternoon	evening	reddish brown olive cast	dark slate	brown	hyaline	olive	3	2	2
hageni	Olive Dun	W	8–9	fast	Mid-July to August	morning	morning and evening	brownish olive	medium gray	brown	hyaline	brown	3	2	2
morrisoni	Red Dun	W	8–9	slow	May-June	morning	morning and evening	light reddish	medium gray	brown	hyaline	brown	3	2	2

EPHEMERIDAE

Three genera of this family are found in trout streams, *Ephemera, Hexagenia,* and *Potamanthus. Hexagenia* is present in the West and common in the Midwest, while *Potamanthus* is more prevalent in the East. *Ephemera* is more widespread, being common from East to West. The nymphs remain burrowed into the stream bottom, except during the molting periods, which take place up to thirty times before emergence. Nymphs in the aquarium were observed to leave the sand in the bottom, swim about in the water, and then, after molting, rebury themselves. It is this habit that gives the trout a chance at them all year long. They are found in the trout's stomach even in the winter months. Nymphs of this family are moderate to large in size, are characterized by mandibles bearing long tusks and legs flanged for burrowing. Adults are distinguished by their large size and other features of wing venation and hind tarsus, as illustrated in the keys.

EPHEMERA

Three species are included in this genus, *guttulata, varia,* and *simulans. Ephemera guttulata* constitutes the famous Green Drake hatch of the East, while *Ephemera simulans* is called the Brown Drake, or simply Drake Hatch, in Michigan and in Idaho. Nymphs are moderate to large in size, have a deeply forked frontal prominence and mandibular tusks that are smooth and slender. Adults display prominently spotted wings and three tails of equal length.

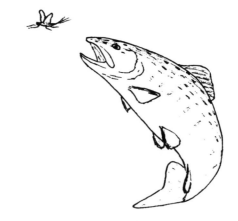

	Locality	Size in mm	Water type	Emergence	Hatch Time	Spinner Fall	Body of Dun	Wing of Dun	Body of Spinner	Wing of Spinner	Body of Nymph	Tails N	D	S
Common Name														
guttulata Green Drake	E	18–22	medium to fast	May 20 to June 15	sporadic and dusk	dusk	yellowish brown marks	grayish olive	light cream	hyaline, dark marks	amber, olive cast	3	3	3
varia Yellow Drake	E M	13–16	medium to fast	June 25 to July 25	dusk	dusk	pale yellow	yellowish gray	pale yellowish olive	hyaline, dark flecks	amber, brown markings	3	3	3
simulans Brown Drake	E M W	10–14	medium to fast	May 25 to July 15	dusk	dusk	yellowish brown marks	gray, brown marks	brown, yellow under	hyaline, brownish black marks	amber, brown markings	3	3	3

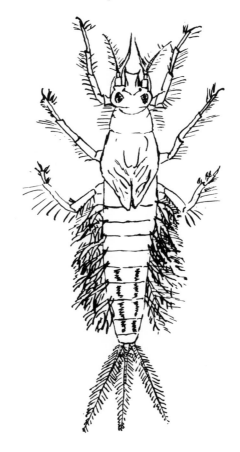

Ephemera

HEXAGENIA

Members of this genus comprise our largest mayflies, with some having bodies up to 1½ inches long. The frontal prominence of the nymph is not forked, as in *Ephemera,* but instead may be rounded, conical, or truncate. Mandibular tusks are long, slender, smooth, and upcurved, with tips divergent. Wings of the adults are not spotted and two tails are present.

Hexagenia limbata

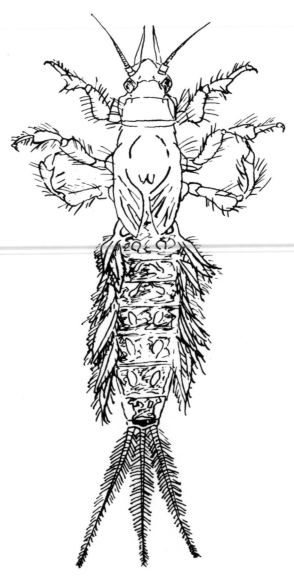

Locality	Common Name	Size in mm	Water type	Emergence	Hatch Time	Spinner Fall	Body of Dun	Wing of Dun	Body of Spinner	Wing of Spinner	Body of Nymph	Tails N D S
limbata	Giant Michigan Mayfly	M 18–33 W	slow	June 20 to July 30	dusk and dark	dusk and dark	yellow, brown marks	gray	yellow, brown marks	hyaline	amber, brown marks	3 2 2

POTAMANTHUS

This genus is represented by only one species, *distinctus,* and is known as the Golden Drake in the East, where it is most common. The nymphs are sprawlers of moderate size and have gills that extend laterally rather than dorsally. Adults are pale in coloration, usually whitish or cream, and have three tails, with the middle one being somewhat shorter than the outer ones.

	Locality	Size in mm	Water type	Emergence	Hatch Time	Spinner Fall	Body of Dun	Wing of Dun	Body of Spinner	Wing of Spinner	Body of Nymph	Tails N D S
												3 3 3
distinctus	Paulinskill E M	13–16	slow	June 20 to July 20	evening	evening	yellowish cream	cream	yellowish cream	hyaline	brown	

Potamanthus

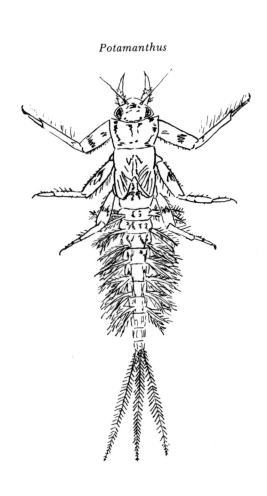

CAENIDAE

The three genera of this family, *Tricorythodes, Brachycercus,* and *Caenis,* constitute our smallest mayflies, with the average size being about 4 mm. Despite their minute dimensions, they are of tremendous importance to the angler. The most significant characteristic of the nymphs are the operculate gills of segment 2, which almost completely cover the ones behind. The nymphs are sprawlers, have three tails and are densely covered with fine hairs. Adults have whitish, well-developed wings, displaying few crossveins and no marginal intercalary veins. The lateral ocelli are very prominent, and hind wings are wholly wanting.

TRICORYTHODES

Members of this genus create some of the best fishing of the season, due mainly to the fact that they occur in fantastic numbers for such a long period of time. Nymphs of *Tricorythodes* have three tails and rather robust bodies, which are covered with fine hairs. The enlarged platelike gills borne by segment 2 are triangular in shape and conceal the gills of segments 3 to 6. Wings of the adult have crossveins and are longer in relation to their width than in *Caenis* and *Brachycercus*. Bodies have a heavy thorax and are usually blackish or dark brown in color. The general coloration gives the impression of a black insect with white wings. Adults have three tails, with those of the male normally being at least three times as long as the body. A pair of small, knoblike projections is located near the back of the head in both sexes.

	Common Name	Locality	Size in mm	Water type	Emergence	Hatch Time	Spinner Fall	Body of Dun	Wing of Dun	Body of Spinner	Wing of Spinner	Body of Nymph	Tails N D S
stygiatus	Tiny White-wing Black	E M	3-4	slow	July 10 to Sept. 30	morning	morning	blackish brown	white	blackish brown	hyaline, whitish	dark brown	3 3 3
atratus	Tiny White-wing Black	E M	3-5	slow	July 20 to Aug. 30	morning	morning	blackish brown	white	blackish brown	hyaline, whitish	dark brown	3 3 3
minutus	Tiny White-wing Black	W	3-6	slow	July 20 to Sept. 30	morning	morning	blackish brown	white	blackish brown	hyaline, whitish	dark brown	3 3 3

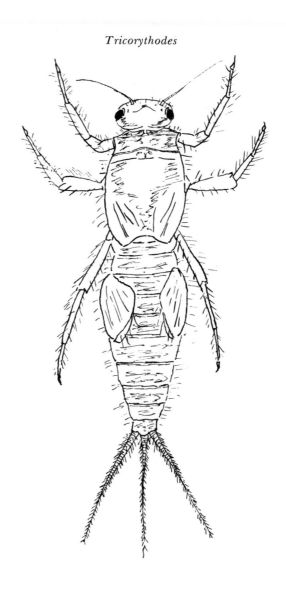

Tricorythodes

BRACHYCERCUS

Nymphs are very similar to *Caenis* except that three prominent conical projections arise from the head, one above the base of each antenna and one over the middle ocellus. Also, as in *Caenis,* the enlarged gills of segment 2 overlap on the midline, but are more rounded on the outer margin. The forelegs are relatively short and separated widely at their base. Adults are a little larger than *Caenis* and a little lighter in color than *Tricorythodes.* The nymphs seem to prefer slower and warmer water than *Tricorythodes,* so they are found less frequently in trout streams.

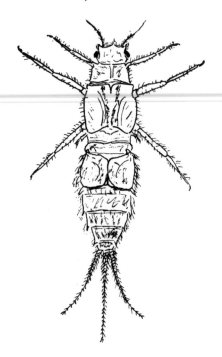

Brachycercus lacustris

	Common Name	Locality	Size in mm	Water type	Emergence	Hatch Time	Spinner Fall	Body of Dun	Wing of Dun	Body of Spinner	Wing of Spinner	Body of Nymph	Tails N D S
lacustris	Tiny White-wing Brown	E M	5–6	slow	July 20 to Aug. 5	morning	morning	olive brown	white	brown	hyaline, whitish	dark brown	3 3 3
prudens	Tiny White-wing Brown	W	5–6	slow	April 1 to Sept. 30	evening	morning	olive brown	white	brown	hyaline, whitish	dark brown	3 3 3

CAENIS

Nymphs of this genus are mainly still-water forms and are, therefore, found to be much more numerous in lakes than in streams. The distinguishing characteristic between the nymphs of *Caenis* and *Tricorythodes* is the shape of the operculate gills on segment 2. In *Caenis*, they are quadrangular rather than triangular. Lack of the knoblike projections on the head differentiate them from *Brachycercus*. The adult bodies are light in coloration, varying from whitish, to buff, to yellowish. Their wings have fewer crossveins than the other genera.

LEPTOPHLEBIIDAE

Two genera of this family, *Leptophlebia* and *Paraleptophlebia,* are found in trout streams and are of importance to the angler. The nymphs have three tails of equal length which are longer than the body and have hair on both sides. The antennae are longer than the thorax and head combined. Bodies are not strongly flattened and display gills that are very noticeable, being either double platelike or deeply forked. Probably the best method for recognizing the adults is to study the wing venation. In the fore wing, Cu_2 is sharply bent and there are no long intercalary veins between M_2 and Cu_1. Three tails are maintained and the size range is 6 to 12 mm.

LEPTOPHLEBIA

This genus contains two important species, *cupida,* which is common to the East and Midwest, and *johnsoni,* which is found in the West. The nymphs have double, platelike gills with long filamentous extensions on abdominal segments 2 to 7 and gills that are deeply forked on the first segment. One peculiar characteristic of the nymphs is their habit of upstream migration prior to hatching. Large numbers have been known to travel as far as a mile, moving along the bank in quiet water. In the adult stage, the middle tail is shorter than the outer ones, wing venation is very distinctive, and bodies are robust.

Caenis simulans

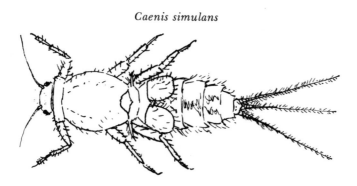

	Common Name	Locality	Size in mm	Water type	Emergence	Hatch Time	Spinner Fall	Body of Dun	Wing of Dun	Body of Spinner	Wing of Spinner	Body of Nymph	Tails N	D	S
johnsoni	Iron Blue Dun	E	6–8	dead to slow	June 10 to July 5	morning	evening	olive brown	slate	light gray	hyaline	brown, yellow under	3	3	3
cupida	Black Quill	E M	10–12	dead to slow	Apr. 25 to Aug. 15	midday and afternoon	afternoon	brown	slate	reddish brown	hyaline	dark brown	3	3	3

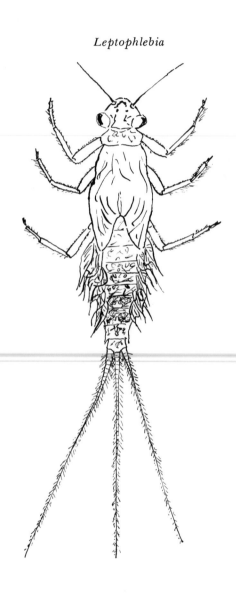

Leptophlebia

	Common Name	Locality	Size in mm	Water type	Emergence	Hatch Time	Spinner Fall	Body of Dun	Wing of Dun	Body of Spinner	Wing of Spinner	Body of Nymph	Tails N	D	S
adoptiva	Slate-wing Mahogany Dun	E M	7–9	medium	Apr. 20 to June 15	afternoon	afternoon and evening	reddish brown	slate	reddish brown	hyaline	dark brown	3	3	3
debilis	Dark Blue Quill	E M W	7–9	slow to medium	Aug. 1 to Oct. 15	afternoon	afternoon	brown	slate	reddish brown	hyaline	brown, yellow under	3	3	3
packi	Dark Blue Quill	W	7–9	medium	July 25 to Aug. 30	sporadic	sporadic	grayish olive	slate	gray, brown rings	hyaline	brown, yellow under	3	3	3
heteronea	Dark Blue Quill	W	7–9	fast	June 2 to Aug. 25	morning	evening	brown	slate	brown	hyaline	brown, yellow under	3	3	3

PARALEPTOPHLEBIA

Nymphs of this genus have slender bodies and gills on segments 1 to 7 that are deeply forked. The head of the nymph is squarish and the middle tail is as long as, or slightly longer than, the outer ones. They are found in similar habitats to those of *Leptophlebia,* but can endure faster currents. Adults have slender bodies and three tails about equal in length and thickness. Often the mating flights will form over open areas away from the stream.

Paraleptophlebia

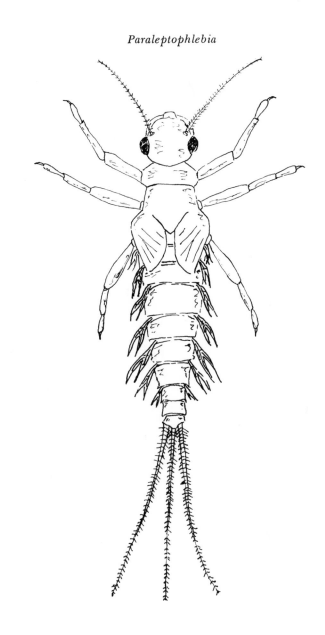

Paraleptophlebia

The identification of mayfly nymphs and adults down to the genus level is easily accomplished by the use of simple keys and an elimination process. To identify the exact species, much closer study is required in conjunction with the keys to the species as found in various books on entomology. Some of the more important publications used in our study include *Mayflies of Michigan Trout Streams* by Justin W. and Fannie A. Leonard, *Aquatic Insects of California* by R. L. Usinger, *The Mayflies of Illinois* by B. D. Burks, and *Mayflies of Utah* by G. F. Edmunds, Jr. The following keys to the families and genus are from *Mayflies of Michigan Trout Streams* by Justin W. and Fannie A. Leonard. For our work, we have chosen the system of classification used by Dr. Leonard as this seems to be the most logical and practical from the angler's point of view.

KEYS TO FAMILIES AND GENERA

Families

NYMPHS

1. Legs flanged for burrowing; mandibles bearing long tusks_____ Ephemeridae
1. Legs cylindrical or flattened in cross section; mandibles without long tusks_____2
2. Gills of abdominal segment 2 operculate, almost entirely covering remaining gills_____Caenidae
2. Gills of abdominal segment 2 absent or, if present, not operculate____3
3. No gills on segments 1–2 (in some cases, 1–3)_____Ephemerellidae
3. Gills on segments 1–7 or 1–6_____4
4. Gills on segments 1–6 (largely concealed by carapacelike extension of mesonotum)_____Baetiscidae
4. Gills on segments 1–7_____5
5. Body strongly flattened; eyes on dorsal surface of head___Heptageniidae
5. Body not strongly flattened_____6
6. Tails clothed with short hairs on both sides_____Leptophlebiidae
6. Outer pair of tails with hairs on inner (mesal) sides only_____7
7. Front tarsal claw double_____Ametropidae
7. Front tarsal claw single_____Baetidae

IMAGOS

1. Lateral ocellus nearly one-half as large as compound eye_____Caenidae
1. Lateral ocellus only one-tenth to one-fourth as large as compound eye__2
2. Abdominal segments 6 and 7 wider, longer, and higher in profile view than segments 5 and 8_____Baetiscidae
2. Abdominal segments 6 and 7 not wider, and not higher in profile view, than segments 5 and 8_____3
3. Hind tarsus with five clearly differentiated, movable segments _____Heptageniidae
3. Hind tarsus with only three or four clearly differentiated segments____4
4. Vein M_2 of fore wing sharply bent near the wing base, running parallel with Cu_1 in this area_____Ephemeridae
4. Vein M_2 not bent, not parallel with Cu_1 near wing base_____5

5. Fore wing with one or two long intercalary veins between
   M$_2$ and Cu$_1$_____4_____Ephemerellidae
5. Fore wing without long intercalary veins between M$_2$ and Cu$_1$_____6
6. Tails three_____Leptophlebiidae
6. Tails two (middle tail vestigial)_____7
7. Fore wings with one or two pairs of long parallel cubital intercalary
   veins and without free marginal veinlets_____Ametropidae
7. Fore wings with either a series of short, slightly sinuate veinlets
   between Cu$_1$ and inner margin of wing, or with one or two
   long, basically detached cubital intercalary veins accompanied
   by free marginal veinlets_____Baetidae

Genera

NYMPHS

Ephemeridae
1. Frontal prominence of head deeply forked_____Ephemera
1. Frontal prominence of head rounded_____Hexagenia

Caenidae
1. Operculate gills of abdominal segment 2 triangular_____Tricorythodes
1. Operculate gills not triangular_____2
2. Operculate gills with inner margins overlapping, outer margins
   rounded; head with prominent tubercles_____Brachycercus
2. Operculate gills nearly rectangular, not overlapping at inner
   margins; head without tubercles_____Caenis

Ephemerellidae
   (In Michigan this family contains but one genus_____Ephemerella)

Baetiscidae
   (This family contains but one genus_____Baetisca)

Leptophlebiidae
1. Gills of abdominal segment 1 deeply cleft, of segments 2–7 broad,
   platelike, with long apical extensions_____Leptophlebia
1. Gills of abdominal segments 1–7 alike, deeply cleft____Paraleptophlebia

Baetidae
1. Gill tufts at base of maxillae and at foreleg bases_____Isonychia
1. No gill tufts at base of maxillae or foreleg bases_____2
2. Posterolateral angles of abdominal segments prolonged as
   thin, flat spines_____Siphlonurus
2. Posterolateral angles of abdominal segments not prolonged
   as spines_____3
3. Gills single_____4
3. Gills double or, if single, bearing a recurved flap_____6
4. Hind wing pad absent_____Pseudocloeon
4. Hind wing pad present_____5
5. Middle tail as long as outer tails_____Centroptilum
5. Middle tail shorter than outer tails_____Baetis

6. Hind wing pad present_____Callibaetis
6. Hind wing pad absent_____Cloeon

Ametropidae
1. Maxillary palp two-segmented_____Metretopus
1. Maxillary palp three-segmented_____Siphloplecton

Heptageniidae
1. Gills of abdominal segment 7 slender, fingerlike_____Stenonema
1. Gills of all segments platelike_____2
2. Gills of abdominal segments 1 and 7 enlarged, each pair
   converging beneath the abdomen to form, with other
   gills, an adhesive disk_____Rhithrogena
2. Gills in normal position, not modified as above_____3
3. Tails two_____Epeorus
3. Tails three_____Heptagenia

Adults

Ephemeridae
1. Wing membrane heavily spotted_____Ephemera
1. Wing membrane not spotted_____Hexagenia

Caenidae
1. Crossveins numerous; male claspers three-segmented, the
   last segment rounded_____Tricorythodes
1. Crossveins very few; male claspers one-segmented,
   sharply pointed_____2
2. Prosternum twice as broad as long; bases of forelegs
   widely separated_____Brachycercus
2. Prosternum twice as broad as long; bases of forelegs
   close together_____Caenis

Ephemerellidae
   (In Michigan this family contains but one genus_____Ephemerella)

Baetiscidae
   (This family contains but one genus_____Baetisca)

Leptophlebiidae
1. Length, 10–12 mm; body robust_____Leptophlebia
1. Length, 4–8 mm; body slender_____Paraleptophlebia

Baetidae
1. Gill remnants present on base of forelegs_____Isonychia
1. Gill remnants absent_____2
2. Hind tarsus with four well-defined segments_____3
3. Both fore and hind wings with numerous crossveins_____Callibaetis
3. Fore wing with few crossveins; hind wing, if present, with
   few or no crossveins_____4
4. Hind wing present_____5
4. Hind wing absent_____6
5. Marginal veinlets of fore wing single_____Centroptilum

5. Marginal veinlets of fore wing in pairs_____Baetis
6. Marginal veinlets of fore wing single_____Cloeon
6. Marginal veinlets of fore wing in pairs_____Pseudocloeon

Ametropidae
1. Fore wing with one pair of cubital intercalary veins; wing
   membrane unspotted_____Metretopus
1. Fore wing with two pairs of cubital intercalary veins; wing
   membrane spotted_____Siphloplecton

Heptageniidae (males only)
1. First segment of fore tarsus as long as second, or longer_____Epeorus
1. First segment of fore tarsus shorter than second_____2
2. Crossveins in stigmatic area of fore wing joined
   in a network_____Rhithrogena
2. Crossveins in stigmatic area of fore wing not joined in a network_____3
3. Penes more or less L-shaped_____Stenonema
3. Penes not L-shaped_____Heptagenia

APPENDIX B

Millimeter to Hook Size Guide *

Millimeter	Hook Size
3 mm	28
4 mm	24
5 mm	22
6 mm	20
7 mm	18
8 mm	16
9–10 mm	14
11–13 mm	12
14–18 mm	10
19–22 mm	8
23–26 mm	6
27–30 mm	4
31–34 mm	2

* This is a *guide* only. Different hook models have different shank lengths.

Index

(Flies are indexed under both common and Latin names)